Self-care prevents compassion fatigue

Terri N. Sisk

Abstract

The purpose of this qualitative descriptive study was to explore how domestic violence advocates who work with physically, mentally, sexually or financially abused clients in the Mid-Atlantic region of the United States, described the influence of self-care in the prevention of compassion fatigue. Research question one for this study centered on what self-care techniques do domestic violence advocates describe as typically being used in the prevention of compassion fatigue. Whereas, research question two asked how domestic violence advocates use self-care to prevent compassion fatigue. The sample for this study were domestic violence advocates who worked at domestic violence organizations in the Mid-Atlantic region of the United States. The theoretical framework utilized for this study was Dorothea Orem's theory of self-care. Interviews and a focus group served as data collection instruments, with thirteen participants engaged in semi-structured interviews, and six participants in the focus group for a total of nineteen study participants. Thematic analysis was utilized to analyze the data collected for this study. The results described the role that boundaries, self-awareness, colleague/organizational care, holistic well-being, the influence on victims, quality of professional life and self-care techniques, play in the prevention of compassion fatigue in domestic violence advocates. Future research should explore the role that organizational culture and leadership styles play in the self-care and compassion fatigue of domestic violence advocates.

Keywords: Domestic Violence Advocates, Self-care, Compassion Fatigue

Dedication

I dedicate this study to my beautiful mother, Glady May Ferguson Osbourne. I am grateful for the loving foundation you provided me. While you did not get to see the conclusion of this part of the journey, it was your steadfast encouragement, spiritual guidance and prayers that empowered me to pursue and remain on this course. Thank you for so beautifully modeling how to be gracious, resolute and resilient. To my beloved husband Micah, and erudite daughter Maylin, I could not have done this without you, you never ever let me give up, I'm so very grateful for you both. To the Domestic Violence Advocates who participated in this study, thank you for your willingness to share your story and highlight an often-unrecognized profession that saves lives and brings hope to the hopeless. Above all, to the Omniscient and Omnipotent one, Lord God Almighty Jesus Christ, you do miracles so great, I would not have made it this far without you. Thank you for how you have led me, I am forever indebted, thank you Lord.

Acknowledgments

To my amazing husband Micah Chavers, words cannot fully encapsulate the incredible support you have given to me throughout this process. You have been accepting of the many sacrifices made, filling in the gaps while ensuring our family had everything we needed. I could not have done this without you, my thank you truly is infinitesimal in comparison to the depths of gratitude I have for your unwavering support. Maylin, it is an honor to have you as my daughter, you have been a source of immeasurable encouragement. Thank you for being the best cheerleader any scholar could have. I hope I have been able to model to you that with steadfast persistence there is no limit to Christ-centered goal attainment. Thank you to my Father, Siblings, especially Elisa, Nieces, Nephew, In-Loves, Cousins and all my family members, I'm grateful for your support. To my extended village and dearest friends who checked in, prayed and encouraged me throughout out this process, please accept my thanks in abundance. To my mentor, Jeffery Thomas, I have been blessed by your prayerful support, thank you for all that you have done for me. Dr. Sylvette LaTouche-Howard, thank you for inspiring me and providing wise counsel throughout the research process. Dr. Shawn Anderson, I am very appreciative of your guidance which helped me to endure, for this I am truly grateful. Dr. Brian Kelly, as my Chair, thank you for your leadership and support in helping me to cross the finish line. To my Methodologist, Dr. Jay Avella, I am thankful for your insight and the vital role you played in helping this study come to fruition. Dr. Kesslyn Brade-Stennis, as my Content Expert, the enlightenment and motivation you provided helped me to become imbued with the persistence needed to accomplish this goal, you are truly appreciated.

Table of Contents

List of Tables xiii

Chapter 1: Introduction to the Study 1

    Introduction 1

    Background of the Study 2

        Historical Background of the Problem 3

        Justification of Gap 4

    Problem Statement 5

    Purpose of the Study 8

    Research Questions 11

    Advancing Scientific Knowledge and Significance of the Study 12

    Rationale for Methodology 14

    Nature of the Research Design for the Study 16

    Definition of Terms 19

    Summary and Organization of the Remainder of the Study 21

    Assumptions, Limitations, Delimitations 24

Chapter 2: Literature Review 27

    Introduction to the Chapter and Background to the Problem 27

        Organization of Literature Review 28

    Background to the Problem 29

        Compassion Fatigue 30

        Self-Care 31

    Identification of the Gap 33

    Theoretical Foundations and Conceptual Framework 37

  Review of the Literature 40

    Compassion Fatigue..41

    Professions Exposed to Compassion Fatigue 44

    Negative Impact of Compassion Fatigue..45

    Domestic Violence..48

    Domestic Violence Overview...49

    Domestic Violence Advocacy 54

    Self-Care Strategies 61

    Methodology...66

    Instrumentation 67

  Summary...69

Chapter 3: Methodology 72

  Introduction..72

  Statement of the Problem...73

  Sources of Data..75

    Interviews..75

    Focus Group..77

    Expert Panel Validation and Field Testing...78

  Research Questions..81

  Research Methodology 83

  Research Design...86

    Unit of Analysis & Unit of Observation...88

  Population and Sample Selection...91

  Ethical Considerations 93

- Trustworthiness 95
  - Credibility 95
  - Transferability 97
  - Dependability 98
  - Confirmability 99
- Data Collection and Management 99
  - Interviews 104
  - Focus Group 108
- Data Analysis Procedures 112
  - Interviews and Focus Group 114
- Limitations and Delimitations 117
  - Limitations 117
  - Delimitations 118
  - Assumptions 119
- Summary 120
- Chapter 4: Data Analysis and Results 123
  - Introduction 123
    - Important Changes and Updates to Information in Chapters 1-3 124
  - Preparation of Raw Data for Analysis and Descriptive Data 127
  - Data Analysis Procedures 134
    - Reflexivity Protocol 135
    - Data Analysis Steps 136
    - Step One: The familiarization of the Data 138
    - Step Two: Generation of Initial Codes 139
    - Step Three: Search for Themes 142

Step Four: Review of Themes 145

Step Five: Defining and Naming Themes 146

Step Six: Production of the Report 148

Trustworthiness 149

Results 150

Presenting the Results 150

Research Question 1 152

Research Question 2 163

Reflexivity Based on Thematic Analysis 172

Summary 173

Chapter 5: Summary, Conclusions, and Recommendations 177

Introduction and Summary of Study 177

Summary of Findings and Conclusion 178

Overall Organization 178

RQ1 179

RQ2 183

Research Questions Answered Based on Study Findings 186

Describing the Phenomenon 187

Reflection on the Dissertation Process 189

Implications 191

Theoretical Implications 192

Practical Implications 193

Future Implications 195

Strengths and Weaknesses of Study 196

Strengths 196

> Weaknesses 197
Recommendations 198
> Recommendations for Future Research 199
> Recommendations for Future Practice 200

List of Tables

Table 1 Semi-Structured Interview Dataset 129

Table 2 Focus Group Dataset 130

Table 3 Study Participant Location & Advocate Title 132

Table 4 Example of the Development of Codes from Participant Responses 140

Table 5 Example of Codes Development into Grouped Category and Category 142

Table 6 Group Category to Category 144

Table 7 Development of Theme from Research Question, Code to Category 146

Table 8 Named Themes 148

Table 9 Summary of Group Category, Category and Themes by Research Question .. 151

Table 10 RQ1 Themes 153

Table 11 RQ2. Themes 164

Chapter 1: Introduction to the Study

Introduction

Domestic violence advocates are exposed to the trauma experienced by their clients (Killian, 2017). As a result, advocates are susceptible to experiencing compassion fatigue by the very nature of their profession (Butler, Carello, & Maguin, 2017). According to Benuto, Yang, Ahrendt and Cummings (2018), compassion fatigue in domestic violence advocates can result in poor mental health, which can manifest in exhaustion, hypervigilance, avoidance, and numbing (p.2). Domestic violence advocates provide a myriad of supportive services and resources to victims (Benuto, Yang, Ahrendt, & Cummings, 2018; Richards & Gover, 2016), with the aim of bringing about domestic violence awareness and ameliorating the trauma experienced by victims. However, the on-going exposure domestic violence advocates experience can deleteriously impact the work that advocates do to assuage the issues experienced by those they serve.

To prevent compassion fatigue domestic violence advocates must intentionally engage in opportunities that will promote optimal holistic functioning. According to Sorenson, Bolick, Wright, and Hamilton (2016), self-care is considered the most significant preventative measure against the development of compassion fatigue. Many professionals in the helping field deploy these measures in order to facilitate the care they disseminate to those who are in need. However, Cocker & Joss (2016), recommend that future research focus on the impact of compassion fatigue interventions in a diverse range of occupation groups exposed to compassion fatigue.

With the prevalence of domestic violence (Macy, Martin, Nwabuzor Ogbonnaya & Rizo, 2018), the work and beneficence of advocates are essential to societal salubrity.

In an effort, to adapt and build resiliency, domestic violence advocates must practice techniques that will aid in their well-being while concurrently facilitating this noteworthy work. However, Salloum, Kondrat, Johnco and Olson (2015), report there is limited empirical information and evidence on the benefits of self-care interventions. To gain greater insight into the efficacy of self-care intervention on this population, further research would elucidate the verifiability of this practice by domestic violence advocates.

To effectuate this research a qualitative descriptive study was facilitated to explore the influence of self-care in the prevention of compassion fatigue in domestic violence advocates in the mid-Atlantic region of the United States. This chapter provides an overview of this research to include information on the background of the study, the resulting problem statement and purpose for this study. In addition, this chapter features the research questions this study sought to answer including how knowledge would be advanced and the significance this study would play within the realm of research. The methodology for this study is featured along with the design utilized to include definitions for keywords and the various assumptions and limitations for this study.

Background of the Study

Domestic violence is a major public health epidemic and a critical issue for leaders of healthcare that warrants support for those who provide services to this population. Domestic violence advocates serve on the front line engaging those who are traumatized by relational violence. Macy, Martin, Nwabuzor Ogbonnaya and Rizo (2018) indicate that within the United States there are 5 million reports of women being abused annually, and that the epidemic of abuse is a tremendous concern within the realm of public health (p.28). In order to diminish this epidemic, domestic violence advocates provide services to domestic violence survivors (Postmus, Hoge, Breckenridge, Sharp-Jeffs & Chung, 2018). As a result of their dedication and support during victim crisis, domestic violence advocates, in turn, expose themselves to compassion fatigue, due to acute and chronic interactions with trauma survivors (Sansbury, Graves & Scott, 2015). Research has indicated that self-care interventions are an important (Bressi & Vaden, 2017) vehicle for promoting worker well-being and have the potential to reduce compassion fatigue (Cocker & Joss, 2016). In order to address this tremendous health epidemic, leaders within health organizations need to safeguard and provide support to domestic violence advocates, as they render aid to those impacted by domestic violence.

Historical Background of the Problem

Research within the broad area of literature began to manifest in the 1970's as feminists began advocacy to classify domestic violence as a human rights issue and not merely an issue between husband and wives needing to cool down (Clark, 2011, p.194). In the literature, domestic violence once was considered a private issue that was confined within the walls of the family unit, and now it has grown to be a complicated issue with grave societal implications (Richard & Grover, 2018). Survivors often receive support and safety from local shelters, organizations proven to be beneficial (Arroyo et al. 2015) to survivors, that emerged as the Battered Woman's Movement in the 60's and 70's to provide survivors with wraparound services in a team decision making capacity (Hackett, McWhirter & Lesher, 2016; Slattery & Goodman, 2017). Research then began to focus on the burn-out experienced by helping professionals (Sprang, Clark & Whitt-Woosley, 2007), characterized by Figley as a byproduct of working with clients who experience trauma (Killian, 2017).

The literature began to grow to incorporate similar concepts with different names such as vicarious trauma (Sabo, 2006), secondary traumatic stress and eventually compassion fatigue (Sprang, Clark & Whitt-Woosley, 2007). Out of the field of psychology, researchers Pines and Maslach (Yip, Mak, Chio & Law, 2017), observed that the worldview of those who observed suffering, also suffered subsequently developing compassion fatigue. The next major area of research that evolved focused on self-care to address the negative effects of providing help to the victimized. Literature reveals that self-care strategies are the most efficacious in diminishing the effects of compassion fatigue (Nelson, Hall, Anderson, Birtles & Hemming, 2018). Current research on compassion fatigue and this population, introduces compassion satisfaction as a positive by-product of working with victims (Singer, Cummings, Boekankamp, Hisaka & Benuto, 2019) along with the exploration of post-traumatic growth (Kometiani & Farmer, 2019).

Justification of Gap

Organizations across the United States deploy Domestic Violence Advocates to provide supportive services to victims of domestic violence. Domestic violence advocates bear witness to the trauma experienced by those they serve and can experience compassion fatigue. This phenomenon was highlighted by Slattery and Goodman (2009) who examined secondary traumatic stress in a diverse spectrum of human service professionals who identified as domestic violence advocates. Therault, Isenor and Pascal (2015), affirmed there was a plethora of information within the mental health field related to compassion fatigue and the detrimental impact it has on workers.

While it was recommended that self-care practices are utilized to treat compassion fatigue (Cocker & Joss, 2016) empirically there is limited data on effective interventions that can aid in diminishing the effects of compassion fatigue. While there is research on self-care strategies for helping professionals, such as nurses (Mills, Wand, Fraser, 2015), police officers (Andersen, Papazoglou, Koskelainen, Nyman, 2015), therapists (Therault, Isenor, Pascal, 2015), child welfare workers (Salloum, Kondrat, Johnco, Olson, 2015) and even funeral directors (McCormack, 2015), there was little literature that correlates self-care practices and effectiveness for those professionals who provide domestic violence advocacy. The gap defined by the above literature focused on how domestic violence advocates who work with physically, mentally, sexually or financially abused clients in the Mid-Atlantic region of the United States, described the influence of self-care in the prevention of compassion fatigue.

Problem Statement

It was not known how self-care influences the prevention of compassion fatigue in domestic violence advocates who work with clients who are physically, mentally, sexually or financially abused. As such, the general population identified in this are domestic violence advocates. The consequence of caring for the traumatized can have a significant deleterious impact on advocates, resulting in numerous negative issues (Alani & Stroink, 2015). Domestic violence advocates are repeatedly exposed too and witness the trauma of clients that they serve, and their unyielding desire to help the suffering can result in compassion fatigue (Kiley, Sehgal, Neth, Dolata, Pike, Spilsbury & Albert, 2018). This phenomenon has a wide-ranging impact on the advocates' ability to function at their peak. Sansbury, Graves and Scott (2015), report that 8% of Americans will experience some form of trauma in their lives, however, the statistics are 15-50% greater for those in helping professions. Subsequently, compassion fatigue sets in which can result in emotional exhaustion, employee turnover and in some cases a diagnosis of post-traumatic stress disorder (Kiley et al. 2018).

Compassion fatigue has far-reaching and devastating consequences not only on the advocate but the organization they serve, the clients they advocate for and society. According to Pfaff, Freeman-Gibb, Patrick, DiBiase and Moretti (2017), helping professionals actively and continuously listen to the horrific and traumatic stories of clients they serve and then seek to give of themselves to empower and restore clients in need. This concentric and on-going giving of self, returned with continuous exposure to trauma, can result in damage to the helper's psyche. Within literature this phenomenon has even been touted as an occupational hazard (Kiley, Sehgal, Neth, Dolata, Pike, Spilsbury & Albert, 2018), to such a degree that the *Diagnostic and Statistical Manual of Mental Disorders (DSM-5)* even qualifies this pervasive exposure to trauma by professionals in the helping field, as a diagnosable stressor within the realm of Post - Traumatic Stress Disorder (Hensel, Ruiz, Finney & Dewa, 2015).

Challenges faced by helping professionals extend beyond themselves and can also impact the organizations where they render services. The cost to organizations impacted by compassion fatigue results in a loss of productivity costing billions of dollars annually (Gerard, 2017). The deleterious financial impact of compassion fatigue can also result in diminished staff retention, increase sick leave and worker disengagement (Adimando, 2017), all of which can contribute to the decreased fulfillment of organizational objectives. Houston-Kolnik et al. (2017), recognized the need for organizations to implement intentional support for workers exposed to secondary trauma, due to the overall decreased productivity, clinical mistakes and poor service planning (Cetrano et al.

2017), often demonstrated by helping professionals who work with traumatized clients. If work performance suffers due to workers experience with compassion fatigue, then the entire organization can be negatively impacted, subsequently, detracting from organization outcomes and objectives to deliver service to those most in need. Hensel, Ruiz, Finney and Dewa (2015) affirm that the working lives of those affected by compassion fatigue also deleteriously encompasses the quality of care delivered.

Domestic violence professionals are not the only casualties of compassion fatigue, as clients also bear the residual effects of the compassion fatigue experienced by advocates. Professionals in the field of domestic violence advocacy, have a reduced capacity to stand underneath the weight of client trauma (Cetrano et al. 2017), to listen and be fully engaged, which repudiates the expectations and functions of those in the helping field. Instead of receiving the support they need, clients will interface with helpers who are emotionally exhausted, demonstrate reduced empathy, exhibit functional impairment and difficulty performing tasks, ultimately resulting in the client experiencing dissatisfaction with services rendered (Kiley et al. 2018; Centrano et al. 2017; Hensel 2015; Sansbury et al. 2015; Pfaff et al. 2017). Based on the deficiencies that manifest from compassion fatigue, clients who have already experienced traumatic and life-altering challenges, in turn, are neglected (Mills, Wand & Fraser, 2015), by the very professionals they seek help from.

Promoting worker well-being through self-care is vitally important in the helping field (Bressi & Vaden, 2017) to diminish burn-out and worker dissatisfaction (Merchant & Whiting. 2015). Even when helpers implement minimal self-care activities, when combined with high levels of distress related to working with traumatized people, they can still experience compassion fatigue (Loolo, 2016). Due to the prevalence of domestic violence (Munoz, Brady & Brown, 2017), domestic violence advocates are needed to support and provide resources to domestic violence victims. Ensuring the wellbeing of domestic violence advocates, through self-care (Alani & Stroink, 2015), is paramount to advocates being able to comprehensively and efficaciously assist this growing population of domestic violence victims. While research has touted self-care practices as advantageous against the harmful effects of working with traumatized individuals, there was minimal empirical literature (Salloum, Kondrat, Johnco & Olson, 2015) to address the influence of self-care in the prevention of compassion fatigue in domestic violence advocates. By researching how self-care influences the prevention of compassion fatigue in domestic violence advocates, findings can enhance and solidify this profession in providing greater care to those who experience physical, mental, sexual and financial abuse.

Purpose of the Study

The purpose of this qualitative descriptive study was to explore how domestic violence advocates who work with physically, mentally, sexually or financially abused clients in the Mid-Atlantic region of the United States, described the influence of self-care in the prevention of compassion fatigue. The target population for this study were domestic violence advocates who resided in the Mid-Atlantic region of the United States. By the very nature of their work, domestic violence advocates often hear the torrid and traumatic tales of victims exposed to domestic violence. This chronic exposure to trauma (Hensel, Ruiz, Finney & Dewa, 2015) can result in advocates experiencing compassion fatigue. According to Baverstock and Finley (2016), this phenomenon can be described as the helper experiencing severe emotional issues due to reported trauma from clients. Subsequently, self-care strategies may be utilized to combat these levels of emotional and mental stress.

Professional self-care as defined by Bressi and Vaden (2017), is the process of engaging in activities that promote comprehensive and on-going wellbeing, and this practice has been touted as effective in reducing compassion fatigue (Cocker & Joss, 2016). However, data was limited on the impact of self-care in a more diverse range of service providing occupational groups (Cocker & Joss, 2016), including domestic violence advocates (Alani & Stroink, 2015). In addition, the literature on professional experience related to compassion fatigue interventions was collected, but only in reference to whether workers had more than one-year experience within the field (Salloum, Kondrat, Johnco & Olson, 2015). This study adds to the body of knowledge by bringing awareness to another occupational group exposed to compassion fatigue and best practices and perspectives related to their stance on self-care in the prevention of compassion fatigue.

This study extends prior research by examining another population, such as domestic violence advocates. Thériault, Isenor and Pascal (2015), proffer that efforts to place self-care at the forefront of professional agendas is absent from empirical data and specifically there was limited information related to self-care strategies for domestic violence advocates (Alani & Stroink, 2015). Therefore, this research brings to eminence the importance of self-care within helping professions, to include domestic violence advocates, adding another professional group to the body of knowledge. This research contributes to the dearth of literature on which self-care techniques are most widely utilized and to what degree they aid domestic violence advocates, with the hopes that those in this field will utilize these practices to diminish the impact of compassion fatigue. Therefore, domestic violence advocates would be able to provide on-going holistic services to this population by incorporating self-care techniques in their personal lives, to minimize the threat of compassion fatigue that looms large within the field of domestic violence advocates.

In addition, this research contributes to the literature on Orem's Theory of Self-Care. This conceptual framework provides greater insight into how advocates are able to achieve balance in self-regulation (Smith, 2015) through self-care, as outlined in Orem's theory. Orem's Theory originated in response to compassion fatigue within the field of Nursing, (Pfaff, Freeman-Gibb, Patrick, DiBiase & Moretti, 2017; Orem, 1971), however, the challenges related to compassion fatigue and the need for self-care are not only relegated to one specific helping field such as nursing, but this framework can be extrapolated and utilized as an inter-professional construct that impacts all helping professions in spite of specialization. An example of this was the use of this theoretical framework outside of the nursing field and applied within the field of domestic violence by Campbell and Weber (2000) and Campbell, Kub, Belknap and Templin, (1997). By utilizing Orem's Theory of Self-Care outside of the nursing realm and parlaying this framework in research related to domestic violence advocates use of self-care, it helps to expand Orem's Theory to other populations outside of the medical field that are exposed to compassion fatigue.

Research Questions

Within the self-care arena there is a broad spectrum of strategies that helpers can utilize to address the challenges related to compassion fatigue. As it relates to self-care in the prevention of compassion fatigue many questions manifested on the efficacy of this phenomenon to address and support domestic violence advocates. Research was needed to explore best practices related to self-care in correlation with compassion fatigue for domestic violence advocates. This information answers these questions and adds to the body of knowledge to the betterment of these professionals and the fragile population they seek to serve. The phenomenon for this research study explored the influence of self-care on domestic violence advocates in the Mid-Atlantic Region of the United States in the prevention of compassion fatigue.

RQ1: What self-care techniques do domestic violence advocates from the Mid-Atlantic region of the United States describe as typically being used in the prevention of compassion fatigue?

RQ2: How do domestic violence advocates from the Mid-Atlantic region of the United States use self-care to prevent compassion fatigue?

Domestic violence advocates responded by providing data on the various self-care techniques that they utilized in their quest to prevent compassion fatigue in their professional lives. This researcher was able to ascertain which strategies are most widely used and which techniques were rarely used for the sample population studied. These research questions added to the theoretical framework of Orem's Theory of Self-Care, outside of the field of nursing by using this theory within the context of domestic violence advocacy, to gain greater insight into self-care. This information adds to the body of knowledge by addressing the problem of compassion fatigue in this service population. The responses to these research questions serve a purpose in providing a platform to diminish and prevent compassion fatigue.

RQ1 provided insight and knowledge for domestic violence advocates in determining which self-care techniques are most typically used in quelling compassion fatigue in addition to sharing strategies that are least utilized to diminish compassion fatigue. RQ2 explored the influence these typically utilized self-care strategies have in diminishing compassion fatigue as described by research participants. With this knowledge, domestic violence advocates will be able to personally utilize these strategies to enhance their professional and personal objectives. Through this research, more advocates may go straight to the most typically utilized self-care strategies used by research participants, instead of negating self-care habits. These research questions address the literature gap by making known which self-care techniques are typically utilized within this sample population and which they would recommend as "Best Practices" for combatting compassion fatigue.

Advancing Scientific Knowledge and Significance of the Study

This study adds to the body of knowledge related to the influence of self-care in the prevention of compassion fatigue in domestic violence advocates. More directly, this study adds to the body of knowledge by specifically addressing typically implemented self-care strategies utilized by domestic violence advocates, in addition to advancing scientific knowledge related to Orem's Theory of Self-Care in conjunction with this profession. While there was a plethora of information on compassion fatigue, secondary trauma and the need for self-care amongst helping professionals (Houston-

Kolnik et al. (2017). There was limited data on the strategy used for the holistic care of domestic violence advocates, specifically related to compassion fatigue (Alani & Stroink, 2015, Merchant & Whiting, 2015, & Jones (2016). Research findings advance scientific knowledge by elucidating this topic, filling the gap and adding to the body of literature on this subject matter. The data gleaned from this study aid in the development of best practices for this profession, encouraging further research on how best to implement findings. This study provides a gateway for other fringe or not so heavily researched helping professions, to conduct independent studies to ameliorate their field.

This study advances scientific knowledge by applying the theoretical framework of Orem's Theory of Self-Care to another professional field. While Orem's Theory of Self-care has traditionally been utilized within the medical field (Pfaff, Freeman-Gibb, Patrick, DiBiase & Moretti, 2017; Orem, 1971), this construct has also been utilized in domestic violence research (Campbell & Weber, 2000; Campbell, Kub, Belknap & Templin, 1997). Orem's Theory of Self-Care punctuates the belief that every caregiver has the innate ability to maintain their equilibrium, (Hasanpour-Dehkordi, A., Mohammadpour, Rahmati, Shahla, Khosravan, Alami, &Akhond, 2015; Wilson, 2017) and embrace the need for holistic functioning. As a helping profession, domestic violence advocates need to maintain their well-being to function optimally and through this study of self-care, a determination can be made in the most efficacious manner to do so. Subsequently, the projection of Orem's Theory of Self-Care on domestic violence advocacy broadens the scope of this theory outside the confines of the medical field, adding to the body of knowledge related to this theory. This study of domestic violence advocates determined that this theoretical model coincides with the principles that Orem specifies is necessary to achieve self-care (Abotalebidariasari, Memarian, Vanaki, Kazemnejad & Naderi, 2017). This research closes the gap in this research topic and adds rich data in gaining a greater understanding of the most successful self-care strategies utilized by domestic violence advocates.

Rationale for Methodology

The methodology utilized to facilitate this study was qualitative in nature, as this approach was the best platform from which understanding of human behavior and experiences related to this subject matter could be generated. A qualitative approach provided insight and explored trends amongst domestic violence advocates related to compassion fatigue and self-care strategies. Qualitative research is a compilation of multiple approaches to data collection (Gehman, Glaser, Eisenhardt, Gioia, Langley & Corley, 2017) and utilized as a best practice because of its manifold methodologies. According to Bowen (2010), qualitative research encapsulates and analyzes information gathered from within the context of the study. Phillips (2017) states that qualitative research is especially beneficial when there is minimal literature and data on the subject matters, as is the case with this population and self-care techniques due to minimal empirical data on this particular topic. In their research Cocker and Joss (2016), reveal that there was little empirical information pertaining to effective strategies and best practices related to compassion fatigue.

The intent of this research was to add to the limited body of knowledge pertaining to self-care and self-care and compassion fatigue, specifically for domestic violence advocates. According to Barocas, Emery and Mills, (2016), domestic violence is a prevalent complex social problem, and as advocates address the trauma experienced by survivors, this can result in a secondary traumatic response (Sansbury, Graves & Scott, 2015). Literature by Dorociak, Rupert, Bryant & Zahniser (2017), reveal that self-care is a strategy to guard against or diminish compassion fatigue, which was an intentional approach advocates can utilize to address the "cost of caring" (p.1). This qualitative research may have a significant impact on advocates, survivors, and society as a whole, as it addresses this complex social problem from the position of self-care provision for domestic violence service providers.

While many researchers espouse the value of mix-methods research to gain a greater realization of the phenomenon under study and boost readers' confidence in this methodology's results (McKim, 2017), this approach was not considered appropriate for this particular study. Driscoll, Appiah-Yeboah, Salib and Rupert (2007), report that there are challenges with mixed methodologies due to the prohibitive nature and concentration on fixed and quantifiable data, which may restrict the depth and exploration of qualitative material. In addition, this research study did not have a large enough sample size to provide noteworthy statistical analysis typically required of a mixed-method approach (Driscoll, Appiah-Yeboah, Salib & Rupert, 2007). Quantitative research often requires voluminous data (Malterud, Siersma, & Guassora, 2016) and predetermined tools such as surveys (Young et al (2018), in this approach. In contrast, and to further justify this qualitative study, the sample size was small and predetermined tools were not utilized in this methodology.

The findings of this research will be added to the body of literature on self-care and its influence on compassion fatigue for domestic violence advocates. Vital information from this qualitative approach will be gleaned from participants' behavioral constructs, which will contribute to the literature related to self-care best practices for domestic violence advocates. This research can be promulgated to workers, administrators, and organizations, who may be empowered to incorporate research findings and ascribe elements of self-care into the culture of the work they do in the beneficence of domestic violence survivors.

Nature of the Research Design for the Study

A descriptive research design was determined to be the most suitable for this study in evaluating the most typically utilized self-care strategies used by domestic violence advocates and their influence in the prevention of compassion fatigue. The ultimate goal of this descriptive study lies within its name, as this approach sought to describe a particular phenomenon while capturing the characteristics that lie therein (Nassaji, 2015). According to Kim, Sefcik and Bradway (2017), qualitative descriptive studies are considered important and are frequently utilized when research questions seek to answer, "the who, what, and where of events or experiences and gaining insights from informant" (p. 1). In addition, a descriptive research design provided a comprehensive depiction of the phenomenon being studied, as such, Colorafi and Evans (2016), state that this approach enables the formulation of organic responses to how participants may feel about a particular subject matter.

Considered most apropos in the field of social science (Colorafi and Evans, 2016), this design methodology was most fitting to examine and explore advocate behavior within its context. This research aligned with this study design, as qualitative descriptive studies are best utilized in exploring phenomena that are not truly understood (Kim,

Sefcik & Bradway, 2017), which is the implication regarding the influence of self-care in the prevention of compassion fatigue within this target population. With this research design approach, rich and descriptive outcomes manifested from participants' responses based on the sociocultural context from which they were expressed (Magilvy and Thomas, 2009).

While there are a plethora of qualitative research designs available such as ethnography, phenomenological, case study and grounded theory, these designs were not selected for this research study. As it related to the ethnographic and phenomenological research designs, there was no need for this researcher to immerse within the social setting of this population to obtain a first-hand account and lived experience of the sample population (Nag, Snowling & Asfaha, 2016; Flasch, Murray & Crowe, 2017), as is typically the case in those particular research designs. This researcher was more concerned with how domestic violence advocates described their self-care and its influence in the prevention of compassion fatigue. As such, there was no need to be immersed in the environment alongside domestic violence advocates for participant observation of self-care, as domestic violence advocates descriptions of self-care sufficed.

Case study research design did not meet the criteria for this study as reported by Baxter and Jack (2008), the tendency with this approach was to examine broad concepts, research questions and become overly engrossed in data. In addition, although grounded theory was one of the most used in contemporary psychology (Ruppel & Mey, 2015), this approach was deemed ill-suited for this study as there was no need to capture a theory grounded in the data obtained.

In the pursuit to obtain the most appropriate research approach, quantitative research designs such as correlational and experimental methods were reviewed and deemed unworthy for this study. The research questions presented did not call for the use of variables or a hypothesis to contrast, examine or pit against each other. (Turner, Cardinal & Burton, 2017; Baggio & Klobas, 2017). In addition, in this study, there was no data to specifically manipulate, measure and quantify. Subsequently, a qualitative descriptive study best encapsulated the in-depth perspective of participants based on its eclectic multi-data source approach and the ability to glean information within a naturalistic setting and context (Colorafi & Evans, 2016; Nassaji, 2015). As such, a qualitative descriptive study fully met the design criteria for this study and aligned ostensibly with this study's research questions.

To understand the influence of self-care strategies in the prevention of compassion fatigue, the target population for this research were domestic violence advocates. The target sample for this study were domestic violence advocates who were employed in the Mid-Atlantic region of the United States. The sample group consisted of domestic violence advocates who were employed at a Family Violence Organization, the sample was derived from those in leadership positions such as management to staff advocates who work in the shelter with domestic violence victims. The primary data collection tools utilized for this research were interviews and a focus group. Interviews were facilitated via video conference, in order to accommodate participants' availability, whereas the focus group was facilitated at a convenient time and methodology for all participants. For this study, convenience sampling was initiated in order to obtain participants that would be most accessible to this researcher. According to Leiner (2014), this sampling approach has proven to be appropriate within the research arena in testing various theories, as was the case in using Orem's Theory of Self-Care which had not been widely used in the context of domestic violence, therefore the sampling approach was considered efficient and simple to implement (Jager, Putnick & Bornstein, 2017).

This researcher sought to recruit forty domestic violence advocates to participate in this research. In an effort to account for attrition, it was determined that twelve-fifteen (12-15) advocates would participate in interviews and six to eight (6-8) participants in the focus group. There were two different samples from the larger target population, those who participated in interviews would not have the opportunity to participate in the focus group and likewise, those selected for the focus group would not participate in interviews. Subsequently, each sample population was asked the same questions in fulfillment of answering the overarching research questions designated for this study.

Definition of Terms

To obtain a greater understanding of the keywords and terminology utilized within this research study, the following terms were defined; *Compassion fatigue, Domestic violence advocate, Domestic violence, Domestic violence survivor, Secondary trauma, Self-care, Vicarious Trauma.*

Compassion Fatigue. The emotional and physical toll of self-sacrifice in the midst of on-going exposure to the distress of individuals experiencing trauma, and the diminished capacity to self-reinvigorate (Pfaff, Freeman-Gibb, Patrick, DiBiase & Moretti, 2017).

Court Advocates. Provide legal support for victims of domestic violence as they navigate through the court system to include providing information related to protective orders while serving as an intermediary between the victim and the office of prosecution (Camacho & Alarid, 2008).

Domestic Violence. The willful intimidation, through physical, sexual, emotional and financial abuse in a relationship by one partner to control another (Barocas, Emery & Mills, 2016).

Domestic Violence Advocate. Trained service providers who support and empower domestic violence survivors by providing comprehensive services to ensure safety, stability, crisis counseling educational awareness and legal assistance needed to ameliorate the survivor's situation (Frey, Beesley, Abbott & Kendrick, 2017). Advocates work with domestic violence survivors who have experienced physical, mental, sexual and financial abuse (Benuto, Yang, Ahrendt, & Cummings, 2018; Logan & Walker, 2018).

Domestic Violence Survivor. An individual who has survived and is recovering from the trauma of domestic violence experience(s) (Newell, Nelson-Gardell, & MacNeil, 2016).

Hotline Workers. Domestic violence advocates who serve on telephone crisis lines, providing crisis counseling, lethality assessments, safety planning and resource provisions for victims and community members (Colvin, Pruett, Young, & Holosko, 2017; Logan & Robert Walker, 2018).

Secondary Trauma. The acute emotional and physical response to the exposure of trauma from another person, akin to post-traumatic stress disorder (Alani & Stroink, 2015).

Self-care. The intentional approach and engagement in activities that promote and foster holistic physical and emotional well-being (Nevins & Sherman, 2016)

Shelter Case Managers. Advocates who are trained help victims determine goals that need to achieve in order to maintain safety and stabilization (Kunkel & Guthrie, 2016).

Vicarious Trauma. The internal change that occurs within a professional that negatively influences their worldview due to chronic engagement and exposure to the trauma of their clients ((Alani & Stroink, 2015; Sansbury et al. 2015).

Summary and Organization of the Remainder of the Study

This study was designed to ascertain the influence of self-care strategies on domestic violence advocates in the Mid-Atlantic region of the United States. Domestic violence is a tremendous public health epidemic that annually costs the government billions of dollars (Arroyo, Lundahl, Butters, Vanderloo & Wood, 2017). In an effort to reduce or ameliorate this issue, domestic violence advocates provide a sincere service as they seek to empower victims through crisis intervention, counseling, awareness and stability support. Although this work is admirable, it also produces secondary trauma for domestic violence advocates who beat witness to the chronic trauma experienced by this population (Pfaff et al. 2017). This can result in compassion fatigue, which can significantly impede the advocate's ability to do the work of supporting survivors through the challenges they face.

Compassion fatigue can result in depression, absenteeism, lack of empathy and disengagement from services (Koenig, 2017; Andersen et al, 2015; Cetrano, 2017; Chiappo-West, 2017). Through the theoretical framework of Orem's Theory of Self-Care

(Smith, 2015), workers may be intrinsically aware of the need to be self-motivated in self-care opportunities. This qualitative descriptive study was facilitated to explore the influence of self-care in the prevention of compassion fatigue in domestic violence advocates in the Mid-Atlantic region of the United States. Orem's Theoretical framework was commonly utilized within the nursing field (Maslakpak, Shahbaz, Parizad & Ghafourifard, 2018) to address patient self-care needs. However, this theoretical approach has also been utilized outside of the nursing realm, seeking specifically to emphasize wellbeing (Hoy, Wagner & Hall, 2007) and even within the confines of studies related to domestic violence and self-care (Campbell & Soeken, 1999, Campbell & Weber, 2000).

The rationale for this approach was that this research would advance scientific knowledge through the lens of Orem's Theory of Self-Care as it related to self-care of domestic violence advocates. The findings of this research can be added to the body of literature on compassion fatigue, self-care and its influence on domestic violence advocates. In addition, keywords and frequently used terminology were defined, to also include assumptions, limitations and delimitations, that were found in this study. Chapter 2 delves more comprehensively into the subject matter of self-care, the problem statement and the theoretical framework.

In addition to exploring domestic violence and its far-reaching impact on communities at large, this chapter reveals the importance of self-care (Alani & Stroink, 2015) and its benefit towards this population. The remainder of this study provided a comprehensive presentation to answer the research questions this study sought to investigate. The following chapter examines the literature surrounding compassion fatigue, domestic violence advocacy and self-care strategies, to include a thorough review of empirical data and literature on the subject matter (Houston-Kolnik et al. 2017; Macy, Martin, Nwabuzor Ogbonnaya and Rizo, 2018). In addition, an outline of the study's theoretical construct is provided in order to demonstrate alignment with study objectives. The qualitative methodology is examined in particular, why this approach was most suitable for this study. Research questions are presented in conjunction with an overall draft of the research design and sources from which data were gleaned.

Upon completion of interviews and focus groups, data analysis commenced with the trustworthiness of this data verified. In a review of the study, limitations and delimitations (Ellis & Levy, 2009) are further expounded upon in addition to consideration of ethical dynamics that presented within the study. In summary, the remaining chapters entailed the following: Chapter 3 expounded on the methodology utilized to facilitate this research elucidating upon the research questions, research design, population and sample utilized to carry out the research, data collection procedures and ethical considerations for this research. Chapter 4 provides the results of this research and the answers to the research questions posed, along with data analysis procedures. Chapter 5 of this study included a synopsis of the entire study, research findings, recommendations and implications for future research and conclusions.

Assumptions, Limitations, Delimitations

In conducting this research, it was with the recognition that there would be elements that are present but in a diminished capacity, with the knowledge that research is not innately value-free, therefore, it was incumbent on the researcher to make these issues known by identifying them (Ritchie, Lewis, Nicholls & Ormston, 2013). According to Marshall and Rossman (2016), there is no perfect research design; subsequently, throughout the course of this research, there were several assumptions, limitations and delimitations that influenced aspects of this research. In the disclosure of these elements, the integrity of the research is assured as these issues were clearly made manifest and brought to the forefront.

Delimitations referred to the boundaries of the study as imposed and specifically chosen by the researcher that are intentionally omitted in order to ensure the manageability and construct of this research (Ellis & Levy, 2009). Whereas, delimitations were in the purview of the researcher, Pyrczak (2016), reports that limitations are weaknesses that are found within research that goes beyond the control and authority of the researcher and these limitations could potentially impact and call into question the validity of study outcomes. In addition, within the facilitation of research, there are assumptions made, which are principles frequently taken for granted by the researcher, about this research (Lindlof & Taylor, 2017). Being cognizant of these assumptions, limitations and delimitations, was fundamentally and vitally important in recognizing the role each may have played in the probity and integrity of the research conducted.

The assumption is that the findings of this research are of interest within the domestic violence advocate target population and are at least acquainted with a few techniques related to self-care. It was assumed that the majority of staff members would be willing and interested in participating in interviews and a focus group, as requested, and provide transparent and honest responses via this research design approach. In addition, assumptions were made that participants, genuinely wanted to aid in the advancement of scientific knowledge through their responses and that they did not have ulterior motives in the responses they provided for this research study. This study also assumed that participants were aware of and utilized self-care strategies and had the knowledge of and were influenced by compassion fatigue. In addition, another assumption of this study related to whether advocates were actively engaged in self-care strategies and even had a desire to prevent compassion fatigue.

There were several study limitations. Participants for this study were limited to those who work in domestic violence organizations where the study was conducted in the Mid-Atlantic region of the United States, subsequently, excluding those from other domestic violence-related organizations outside of the region. In addition, the organizations where the research was facilitated did not have a large number of staff and therefore the sample size would be small. Within this field, it was a predominantly female-dominated industry and most of the participants were female. Another limitation, were the unknown issues that may have manifested within the organization where the study was conducted and how these undisclosed nuances may have influenced this study. Another factor beyond this researcher's control were the responses provided by participants and whether they were transparent and forthcoming with information needed in facilitating this research.

Delimitations for this study included the following imposed constrictions:

1. Instead of utilizing multiple organizations from which to pull study participants from, this researcher limited where the sample population would come from to initially seeking out domestic violence organizations within the Mid-Atlantic region of the United States. Limiting study participants to organizations in the Mid-Atlantic region, was a delimitation as the use of multiple organizations from across the United States instead of just the Mid-Atlantic region, could have provided greater insight and assorted answers to this study' research question.

2. Another researcher-imposed limitation was the methodological approach that was selected to facilitate this research. This study was limited to a qualitative methodology instead of quantitative approach, which could have obtained data, measurements and outcomes that a qualitative purview would not be able to provide.

3. This researcher sought to exclusively study domestic violence advocates and omitted the perspective of domestic violence survivors of which the responses of survivors, could have provided additional context to this study on self-care in the prevention of compassion fatigue.

4. In the selection of data sources chosen for this study, this researcher opted not to utilize field notes and observations with research participants. These approaches were often seen as intrusive and intense and as such they were deselected from this study in favor of interviews and a focus group.

Chapter 2: Literature Review

Introduction to the Chapter and Background to the Problem

People who work with victims of domestic violence do so at significant risk to themselves. The cost of caring (Pfaff, Freeman-Gibb, Patrick, DiBiase & Moretti, 2017) can have a deleterious impact on those in professions exposed to compassion fatigue, if their holistic well-being is left unattended. Professionals, who demonstrate compassion to those who are disenfranchised do so at a high price to themselves and those they seek to serve. Those who work in the field of domestic violence witness the trauma of domestic violence survivors.

Domestic violence advocates as they are called, are considered to be in a field that is susceptible to the damaging effects of compassion fatigue (Butler, Carello, & Maguin, 2017). According to Fisackerly, Sira, Desai and McCammon (2016), compassion fatigue is an adverse result of exposure to the trauma experienced by those receiving help. It is vitally important for the helper to deploy strategies of self-care to sustain their capacity to demonstrate compassion to those who are vulnerable. One such strategy is the methodology of self-care implementation, which has been touted as most efficacious in combatting the deleterious impact of compassion fatigue.

Literature abounds with data punctuating the need for self-care in helping professions, (Houston-Kolnik et al.2017; Fisackerly et al. 2016, Alani & Stroink, 2015) and the benefits this practice has on helpers. Research on self-care has been conducted on various helping professionals (Mills, Wand, Fraser, 2015; Andersen, Papazoglou, Koskelainen, Nyman, 2015; Therault, Isenor, Pascal, 2015; Saloum, Kondrat, Johnco, Olson, 2015; McCormack, 2015). Domestic violence advocates provide supportive services and resources to victims (Richards & Gover, 2016), with the aim of ameliorating the trauma experienced by victims and bringing about awareness related to domestic violence. Due to the reoccurring exposure to victim trauma, advocates can experience compassion fatigue (Houston-Kolnik et al. 2017; Alani & Stroink, 2015), which can negatively impact the help provided to those who need it most. However, there is limited empirical data related to the efficacy of self-care for domestic violence advocates.

Exploring self-care strategies that advocates may utilize in the prevention of compassion fatigue, can ensure helpers function at their optimal level (Dorociak, Rupert, Bryant & Zahniser, 2017) in providing needed support to domestic violence victims. However, it is not known how self-care influences the prevention of compassion fatigue in domestic violence advocates from the Mid-Atlantic Region of the United States and this study will seek to explore this phenomenon. This study will explore the influence of self-care strategies of domestic violence advocates who work with clients who are physically, mentally, sexually and financially abused, in the prevention of compassion fatigue.

Organization of Literature Review

This chapter is organized into five sections, with each element progressively expounding on the subject matter of this research. First, an in-depth analysis of the background for this study was provided, detailing how domestic violence advocates were prone to compassion fatigue and the role self-care plays in their ability to function professionally. Secondly, the framework for this study was presented, featuring Orem's Theory of Self-Care and the manner in which this construct shaped the parameters and lens from which this study manifests. This chapter also provides an overview of the multilayered issues related to domestic violence, the role of advocates in supporting victims and the need for self-care implementation within this demographic. The fourth section summarized the aforementioned topics to fully synthesize all elements of this research study. Lastly, this section elaborated on the manner in which the study was facilitated, by exploring the research methodology, design capacity and the multimodal data collection tools

To obtain a comprehensive review of the literature, data for this research was gleaned from diversified sources. Reviews were conducted from the following; peer-reviewed empirical articles, dissertations, guest editorials found in scientific journals, websites such as the National Coalition Against Domestic Violence, domesticviolence.org, and data from the World Health Organization. This researcher utilized Grand Canyon University library, the University of Maryland library and Google Scholar to search for information on the following key terminologies; compassion fatigue, self-care, domestic violence, domestic violence advocates, vicarious trauma and Orem's Theory of Self-Care.

Background to the Problem

Due to the limited research found on domestic violence advocates and their self-care strategies, further research was necessitated to contribute to the literature on this topic. Many professionals seek to provide support and empowerment to those who are in trauma and experiencing episodes of crisis. They put their professional expertise into practice and strive to bring help during an acute or chronic life-changing moment in the lives of those they serve. This ongoing contact can result in compassion fatigue, which is the emotional and physical toll of self-sacrifice displayed in the midst of on-going exposure to the distress of individuals experiencing trauma, and the diminished capacity to self-reinvigorate (Pfaff, Freeman-Gibb, Patrick, DiBiase & Moretti, 2017). The impact of compassion fatigue, a form of wear and tear on the helper, impacts their ability to successfully carry out job functions. As a result, the ability for domestic violence advocates to independently invest in their overall wellbeing is vitally important to be able to maintain the professional's capacity to care.

Domestic violence advocates fall in line along with a multitude of helpers who can experience compassion fatigue because of their chronic exposure to traumatized clients (Slattery & Goodman, 2009). Advocates play a critical role in helping to augment the lives of domestic violence survivors (Frey, Beesley, Abbott and Kendrick, 2017) who have experienced any combination of trauma related to physical, mental, sexual and financial abuse (National Coalition on Domestic Violence, 2015). As unfortunate as it is, exposure to trauma can be considered commonplace (Green et al. 2016), yet it brings with it a myriad of consequences (Alani & Stroink, 2015). Over a period of time the phenomenon of compassion fatigue develops (Adimando, 2017; Ludick & Figley, 2017)) and domestic violence advocates would do well to implement measures to remediate these issues.

Compassion Fatigue

Compassion fatigue is a widely used term that has been trending across a spectrum of professions. A literature review facilitated by Coetzee and Laschinger (2018), indicated that the term compassion fatigue originally appeared in the 1990s and in spite of its newness a significant amount of research has been conducted on this phenomenon. It initially figured prominently in the field of nursing based on their chronic exposure to patients who were ill and the need to provide ongoing care (Pfaff et al, 2017, Adimondo, 2017). As proffered by Fisackerly, Sira, Desai, and McCammon (2016), nurses and those in helping professions must demonstrate a certain level of vulnerability as they strive to be empathetic in taking care of those who are ill and experiencing trauma. While nurses and other helping professionals may experience compassion satisfaction (Coetzee & Laschinger, 2018; Pfaff et al, 2017), a sense of fulfillment in their duties, it is more likely that compassion fatigue may set in overtime (Adimondo, 2017).

Self-Care

The literature pertaining to compassion fatigue and the need for self-care abounds with trends related to various professions, who regularly interact with clients who are in crisis. Dorociak, Rupert, Bryant and Zahniser (2017), report in an effort to combat the stress experienced by helping professions, self-care presents as an immeasurable remediating priority. Through the strategic implementation of personal techniques of caring for self (Adimondo, 2017), helping professionals may achieve balance while still providing care to those in crisis. Studies by Pfaff et al, 2017, Andersen et al, 2015; Nevins and Sherman (2016), all concur in the recommendation for further study on self-care strategies, education and awareness, across interdisciplinary helping fields. While there is a preponderance of literature on compassion fatigue (Coetzee & Laschinger, 2018), the converse is true pertaining to self-care modalities, where there is limited empirical data ((Mills et al, 2015; Kiley et al, 2018) available on this phenomenon.

By way of their profession, domestic violence advocates chronically experience exposure to the distress of their clients. Survivors of domestic violence experience a myriad of abuse (Macy et al. 2018), wherein one seeks to control the other through patterns of abuse. According to Richards and Gover (2016), advocates provide a multi-tiered approach to direct services for victims, resource referral and advocacy awareness to domestic violence survivors. While the work done with survivors can be rewarding and empowering resulting in compassion satisfaction (Frey, Beesley, Abbott and Kendrick, 2017), advocates also experience the antithesis of this, in the form of compassion fatigue (Adimando, 2017). In this capacity, advocates also bear witness to the horrific physical and emotional abuse experienced by their clients. This compassionate caring in the face of repeated exposure to trauma may irreparably defile the psyche of the helper altering their worldview (Pfifferling & Gilley, 2000) (Geoffrion, Morselli & Guay, 2016), seeing it as untrustworthy and unsafe. Pfaff et al. (2017), report that "compassion fatigue is now recognized as an interprofessional concern that can affect all helping professions regardless of specialty focus" (p.1). To address this challenge, Nevins and Sherman (2016); Houston-Kolnik, -Ruan and Greeson (2017), Dorociak, Rupert, Bryant & Zahniser (2017) tout the benefit of self-care in the treatment and prevention of compassion fatigue.

While self-care is considered a remedy in the recourse for compassion fatigue, there is a paucity in the literature pertaining to its impact on domestic violence advocates. According to Alani and Stroink (2015), much has been written about self-care in various helping professions, however, very little is intimated within the literature regarding domestic violence service providers. Within the literature there is commensurable research on self-care practices for nurses, police officers, therapists, child welfare workers, and even funeral directors (Mills, Wand, Fraser, 2015; Andersen, Papazoglou, Koskelainen, Nyman, 2015; Therault, Isenor, Pascal, 2015; Saloum, Kondrat, Johnco,

Olson, 2015; McCormack, 2015), however, research on domestic violence advocates is unknown. Subsequently, Cocker and Joss (2016), report the need for research to be facilitated on self-care, as it relates to a diverse range of professions. To further support the need for this present study, Alani and Stroink (2015), reveal that there is less literature present on self-care strategies of domestic violence advocates and states that it may be of interest to explore and understand self-care strategies of those employed in the field of domestic violence.

Studying strategies of self-care on domestic violence advocates would add to the body of literature pertaining to the aforementioned helping professionals. Due to their constant exposure to trauma victims, domestic violence advocates would qualify in the category of being exposed to compassion fatigue (Alani & Stroink, 2015; Slattery & Goodman, 2009). This gap in literature, the noteworthy work of domestic violence advocates and the need to facilitate greater understanding of self-care strategies amongst this population, supports and solidifies the need for further research to contribute to the literature on this topic.

Identification of the Gap

The literature is replete with the benefits of self-care strategies such as health promotion, decreased anxiety, wellness maintenance, a positive outlook on life, stress alleviation and lower levels of burnout and compassion fatigue(Mills, Wand, Fraser, 2015; Colman, Echon, Lemay, McDonald, Smith, Spencer & Swift, 2016; Therault, Isenor, Pascal, 2015; Salloum, Kondrat, Johnco, Olson, 2015; McCormack, 2015). Yet there is a paucity of literature on self-care strategies pertaining specifically to domestic violence advocates, who work with physically, mentally, sexually or financially abused clients. Advocates witness the trauma of domestic violence survivors and are considered a professional group susceptible to the damaging effects of compassion fatigue (Butler, Carello, & Maguin, 2017; Ludick & Figley, 2017). These deleterious experiences not only impact domestic violence advocates but also the organizations they serve and the clients they seek to nurture and support. The consequences of chronic trauma exposure and compassion fatigue can result in diminished productivity, loss of organizational revenue, the development of organizational silence, diminished awareness and poor training (Gerard, 2017; Geoffrion, Morselli & Guay, 2016). Subsequently, organizations that support advocates, can benefit from participating in supporting workers in the deployment of self-care strategies (Wood, 2014) enabling workers to pour back into themselves what has been deleteriously lost due to chronic trauma work.

Cocker and Joss (2016) expose the gap in the literature as it relates to compassion fatigue and the strategies that may be utilized to address and diminish its occurrence. While literature may abound in the nursing field on this subject matter (Marcum, Rusnak & Koch, 2018; Coetzee & Laschinger, 2018; Jarrad, Hammad, Shawashi & Mahmoud, 2018), literature from Cocker and Joss (2016) strongly suggests the need for future research on compassion fatigue in diverse professions beyond the field of nursing, to examine the efficacy of interventions such as self-care to combat compassion fatigue. As it pertains to this research, Merchant and Whiting (2015), suggest that further research on domestic violence advocates, who are considered frontline workers (An & Choi 2017), can result in a greater appreciation for the lived experience of advocates. In addition, Alani and Stroink (2015), support the need for future research on self-care within domestic violence advocates, as these helpers are exposed to compassion fatigue.

Prior research focused primarily on resources and comprehensive support for victims of domestic violence (Richards & Gover, 2018; Hughes, 2017). Only recently has the literature highlighted the deleterious impact of service provision on advocates (Houston- Kolnik, 2017, Alani & Stroink, 2015). Empirical data espouses the benefits of self-care in maintaining a professional and personal balance (Sansbury, Graves & Scott, 2015, Dorociak et al. 2017) as an important function of those providing services to traumatized populations. In the same regard, while the literature may punctuate the benefits of self-care (Sansbury, Graves & Scott, 2015, Newell, Nelson-Gardell, & MacNeil, 2016), specific and comprehensive empirical data on this subject matter pertaining to domestic violence advocates is limited (Alani & Stroink, 2015), and is delved into further in this section.

The literature on the connection between domestic violence survivor and advocate has evolved through the years to reflect the need for advocates to provide customizable treatment methodologies for the survivor instead of a blanket "one shoe fits all" approach previously demonstrated (Goodman, Fauci, Sullivan, DiGiovanni & Wilson, 2016, Macy et al. 2018). As a result of this newfound approach, the knowledge, skills and abilities of domestic violence advocates have expanded (Richards & Gover, 2018), compounding the complexity and intensity of the restorative (Kulkarni, Bell, Hartman and Herman-Smith, 2013) and vital support they provide survivors. Trends within advocacy espouse the need for advocates to provide trauma-informed care, continuous training in service and resource provision and the need for advocates to embrace and utilize self-care methodologies (Sansbury, Graves & Scott, 2015; Stover & Lent, 2014; Cattaneo & Goodman, 2015). In the study conducted by Alani and Stroink (2015), they provided a cursory examination of secondary traumatic stress, emotional exhaustion and burnout and the importance of addressing these factors as it relates to self-care within domestic violence advocates.

Primarily, their research emphasized the manner in which the work facilitated by domestic violence advocates impacts their well-being, barriers to achieving self-care and self-care strategies deployed by this population. Research surrounding the elements related to self-care (Dorociak et al. 2017, Newell, Nelson-Gardell, & MacNeil, 2016) has manifested in juxtaposition to research pertaining to compassion fatigue and secondary traumatic stress. Findings presented by Alani and Stroink (2015) are also supported by data compiled by Alvarez, Fedock, Grace and Campbell (2017) highlighting the need for further training in best practice self-care strategies utilized by advocates, in their care of survivors. In their study, Alani and Stroink (2015) also revealed an interesting trend in the advocates' inability to distinguish between work and self-care, touting that doing more advocacy work with this population was also a form of self-care for the advocate, and not necessarily a contributing factor in the development of compassion fatigue or secondary traumatic stress. This ideology is also supported within the literature elucidating the benefit of compassion satisfaction and vicarious resilience (Frey et al. 2016; Cetrano, 2017; Coetzee & Laschinger, 2018) from working with this population.

In addition, research in this field primarily includes female participants and future research could be conducted from a male advocate perspective to determine if there are differentiations between gender, related to advocating wellbeing and self-care. Subsequently, Wade (2018), recommends more research be facilitated on self-care for helping professionals in the prevention of compassion fatigue. Slattery and Goodman

(2009), indicate that additional empirical investigation is warranted to ascertain the most beneficial work environments for domestic violence advocates. According to Jones (2016), it is beneficial to identify self-care and training for victim advocates and it is recommended that researchers further investigate the self-care strategies utilized by victim advocates. Domestic violence advocates are considered part of the conglomerate of helping professionals impacted by secondary traumatic stress from their client (Benuto, Yang, Ahrendt, & Cummings, 2018; Ludick & Figley, 2017). Above all, Alani and Stroink (2015), propose further research is needed to broaden the conceptualization of self-care (Miller, Donohue-Dioh, Niu & Shalash, 2018) amongst the domestic violence advocacy population.

To further support this study, Merchant and Whiting (2015), indicate there is a plethora of research on domestic violence interventions and strategies but very little research on domestic violence advocates, who are considered frontline workers in this field. Therefore, this research adds to the parse literature related to advocates. In addition, Alani and Stroink (2015), reveal that there is less literature present on self-care strategies of domestic violence advocates and states that it may be of interest to explore and understand self-care strategies of those employed in the field of domestic violence. This study and its findings meet this need and contribute to the literature on self-care strategies of domestic violence advocates working with abused clients in the Mid-Atlantic region of the United States.

Theoretical Foundations and Conceptual Framework

This qualitative descriptive study was facilitated utilizing the theoretical framework of Orem's Theory of Self-Care to explore the influence of self-care in the prevention of compassion fatigue in domestic violence advocates from the Mid-Atlantic region of the United States. Dorothea Orem (Orem, 1971), a renowned nursing scholar, conceptualized the framework of self-care in an effort to aid nursing staff with self-care practices. Orem utilized the tenets of self-care and self-care deficit to outline a greater understanding of an individual's effort to achieve well-being (de Lima, dos Santos, Comassetto, de Oliveira, Correia and da Silva, 2017).

According to Orem (2001), self-care entails engaging in practices that establish the maintenance of life, health and well-being. The individual initiates and is self-motivated in demonstrating the ability to tend to their holistic needs. In doing so, the person becomes the change agent and is also the one who is changed from the initiative of their own innate efforts. The model for this theory stems from the concentric view of self-care, self-care agency and self-care requisites, detailing how human beings manage and address their on-going needs (Renpenning & Taylor, 2011). It was Orem's belief that people engaged in self-care when they were knowledgeable about its premise, in addition to being self-motivated (Abotalebidariasari, Memarian, Vanaki, Kazemnejad and Naderi, 2017) to participate in these self-care activities. The self-motivation to take personal care (Abdollahimohammad, 2018) is a fundamental priority of Orem's Theory of Self-Care, along with decisions that are made to diminish challenges that impede daily living, which are impacted by life experience and knowledge (Carneiro, Lopes, Lopes, Santos, Bachion, & Barros, 2018). Orem's theory delineates that every caregiver has the innate ability to maintain their equilibrium while bearing witness to the burden of their patient's challenges (Mohammadpour, Rahmati, Shahla, Khosravan, Alami, &Akhond, 2015; Wilson, 2017) and embrace the need for holistic functioning.

Research has indicated the need for those in high-risk professions and exposed to trauma to engage in activities of self-care (Houston-Kolnik et al.2017). According to Abotalebidariasari, Memarian, Vanaki, Kazemnejad and Naderi (2017), it is incumbent to self-identify elements that may impinge on the ability to achieve a holistic functioning, these challenges may be remedied through the use of self-care activities and the transformative process of caring for self, through the fulfillment of self-care functioning. In making this choice they have selected to change their internal and external environment through their volition of self-care. In order to provide supportive and engaging services to those who are impacted by domestic violence, advocates must make the decision to care for themselves. While it may appear misaligned to utilize a framework typically used within the field of nursing to address patient self-care needs (Maslakpak, Shahbaz, Parizad & Ghafourifard, 2018), and apply it to the field of domestic violence, this theoretical construct provides alignment across disciplines based on its wide swath of principles related to self-care that this theory proffers and is found within this research.

This theoretical approach has been utilized outside of the nursing realm, seeking specifically to emphasize wellbeing (Hoy, Wagner & Hall, 2007,) and has also been utilized within the confines of studies related to domestic violence and self-care (Campbell & Soeken, 1999, Campbell & Weber, 2000). In their study Campbell & Soeken, (1999), utilized Orem's Theory of Self-Care as a framework to examine the self-care agency of battered women and its influence on their ability to maintain self-care. The findings from this study reveal that exposure to domestic violence can negatively impact self-care abilities. Therefore, increasing self-care aids and supports was deemed an appropriate intermediary to improve wellbeing. Likewise, this research evaluates the relationship between self-care and the prevention of compassion fatigue in workers exposed to the secondary trauma of domestic violence. This research advances scientific knowledge through the lens of Orem's Theory of Self-Care in answering the research questions pertaining to the scope and methodology of self-care that domestic violence advocates utilize in the prevention of compassion fatigue.

The theoretical framework of Orem's Theory of Self-Care aligns with this research study as it sought to highlight the influence of self-care practices on domestic violence advocates (Alani & Stroink, 2015). The construct of this model supports the research questions, pertaining to the influence of self-care in domestic violence advocates in the prevention of compassion fatigue. Understanding advocates' intentionality in choosing to engage in activities that will benefit their self-care through their independent decision-making process can support optimal functioning in their role. Orem (2001) is guided by the practice of activities that will maintain life, health and promote wellbeing and identify which self-care strategies are most successful can help augment principles of well-being within the field of domestic violence advocacy. In addition, identified self-care strategies of advocates underscore Orem's theoretical framework of self-regulation and motivation, by preventing and/or counteracting the effects of compassion fatigue (Adimondo, 2017).

Review of the Literature

This section delves into the empirical data surrounding this research subject matter and seminal literature. A thorough review of research pertaining to the phenomenon of compassion fatigue, the public health epidemic of domestic violence, the role of advocacy in providing support for survivors, the need for and influence of self-care and the strategies utilized to enhance well-being, will be presented.

Compassion Fatigue

Demonstrating empathy in chronic and acute situations can be taxing and result in challenges that may not always be easily remedied. According to Yip, Mak, Chio and Law (2017), the phenomenon of compassion fatigue manifested within the field of psychology by Pines and Maslach who recognized that the worldview of those who observed suffering, also suffered. The literature also posits that compassion fatigue began to manifest in the literature by Johnson in 1992 (Adimondo, 2017), in the examination of burn-out of nurses (Coetzee & Laschinger (2018). it was initially considered an issue that manifested singularly within the healthcare field (Sorenson, Bolick, Wright, and Hamilton 2016), particularly amongst nurses. Compassion fatigue has been trending upwards in the literature amongst other helping professions (Kiley et al, 2018; Fisackerly, Sira, Desai & McCammon, 2016; Cetrano et al. 2017), since that time.

Compassion fatigue has been defined broadly, yet similarly with some researchers within the literature indicating that it is the diminished capacity to manage the suffering of clients (Cetrano et al. 2017), the occupational hazard of caring too much (Yoder, 2010) and the emotional, physical, and work-related effects of providing compassion and empathy to others over a period of time (Adimondo, 2017). In the literature by Alani and Stroink, (2015), a three-layered approach to compassion fatigue manifests resulting in a) emotional exhaustion, (b) negative detachment to others (c) diminished compassion satisfaction and a sense of achievement. Whereas, Killian (2008), proffers the sum of compassion fatigue to rest within the realm of fear and anxiety and Chiappo-West (2017) referenced it to be the negative aspect of helping people.

According to Coetzee and Laschinger (2018), there has been a significant amount of research facilitated on compassion fatigue throughout the world amongst a myriad of professions. In their international mixed methods research on mental health staff, Cetrano et al. (2017), sought to understand the impact of compassion fatigue, burnout and compassion satisfaction on the quality of working life. Similarly, to domestic violence advocates, mental health professionals are considered at risk (Centrano, 2017) for exposure to trauma from their clients. The background of their study brought to the fore the impact of working with traumatized clients upon mental health professionals, ranging from compassion satisfaction, burnout, to compassion fatigue. Each of these variables was defined, with minor differentiations along the spectrum from being rewarding to emotionally exhausting. The gap focused on contributing to literature by combining the variables and including a wide swath of mental health professionals instead of single or dual profession research typically facilitated.

Research questions investigated the extent that the aforementioned variables influenced the quality of working life. The methodology included a cross-sectional study of three all-inclusive mental health organizations, with no distinction between agencies and all staff members invited to participate and complete the 13 measures of Quality Working Life questionnaire, which included demographics as independent variables of the study. The Professional Quality of Life Scale (ProQOL III) construct validity tool was deemed appropriate, consisting of thirty (30) Likert scale items with the dependent variables of compassion fatigue, burnout and compassion satisfaction. Statistical analysis resulted in findings indicating that compassion fatigue and burnout had a high level of impact upon the work-life of mental health professionals and a negative effect on service delivery. Specifically, more concern was placed on the interference of work-life impinging on participant personal life than the converse and environmental factors and their influence on compassion fatigue. Indicators for future research recommended a focus on client perception of professional efficacy, in relation to the study variables and implemented organizational goals to address compassion fatigue, burnout and compassion satisfaction.

Research within the literature has continued to espouse the need for compassion fatigue in awareness and education within diverse professional groups. Similarly, to domestic violence advocates, Fisackerly, Sira, Desai and McCammon (2016), added to the body of literature by researching child life specialists, another group of helping professionals that are not figured prominently within research as it relates to compassion fatigue. Bearing witness to the trauma of clients can be pernicious in nature and even more so when tending to the trauma of children. Council (2006), indicates that child life specialists serve as part of an interdisciplinary team, helping to make comfortable the child who is receiving treatment through taught coping mechanisms and management of their illness. Prior to Fisackerly et al. (2016), there were only two studies that included child life specialists and one where the profession was the sole focus of the study, in which 75% of specialists were at risk for compassion fatigue. This particular study sought to explore the relationship between environmental factors on compassion fatigue and the measurement of compassion fatigue in comparison to health care professions that were previously researched. Participants were 154 certified child life specialists who completed another version of the ProQOL-5, similar to the ProQOL-III completed in the study by Cetrano et al. (2017), a tool that measures risk factors for Compassion fatigue, burnout and compassion satisfaction and quality of life, but not predictors of prevalence of these variables.

Demographic and participant characteristics were coded and categorized by unit (emergency department, pediatric intensive care unit and hematology/oncology) and environmental factors, with a majority of respondents being female and white. Responses ranged from child life specialists experiencing child fatality to satisfaction from patient recovery, with statistical analysis assessing higher risk factors of compassion fatigue and burnout by child life specialists stationed in emergency rooms and those who have observed patient fatalities. This study contributed to the literature on compassion fatigue by highlighting risk factors for these variables within this helping group, noting that risk level increased based on the unit where the helping professional is stationed and the importance of early-career intervention on victim emotional wellbeing. According to Fisackerly et al. (2016), the implications for practice pertaining to this study punctuates the important role that receiving supervisory support has on diminishing the impact of compassion fatigue on child life specialists. In addition, findings for this study highlight the need for further research on compassion fatigue and that acknowledging risk factor identification is a key component in the prevention and remediation of compassion fatigue.

Professions Exposed to Compassion Fatigue

Literature (Sansbury, Graves & Scott, 2015, Ludick & Figley, 2017) reiterates that interfacing with compassion fatigue can be considered an occupational hazard, whether serving as a mental health specialist or working with children who are abused, compassion fatigue across the spectrum of helping professions, needs to be examined to determine prevalence, identify risk factors and prevention. The medical field, particularly the area of nursing (Pfaff et al, 2017; Hensel et al, 2015; Alani & Stroink, 2015; Nevins & Sherman, 2016), is replete with variations of studies related to the impact and influence of compassion fatigue on nurses. In addition, the field of mental health therapists (Centrano, 2017) and social workers (Coetzee, 2017) have also been found to investigate this phenomenon. However, while parse, there are other professionals featured in the literature pertaining to the challenges related to compassion fatigue. From researchers, educators, clergy and doctoral students, the literature on the manifestation of compassion fatigue within diverse professions abound (Noullet, Lating, Kirkhart, Dewey & Everly, 2018; Strosky, Wang, Hill, Long, Davis & Cuthbert, 2018; Koenig, Rodger, & Specht, 2017). While the literature may present a considerable amount of research on compassion fatigue across professional genres, empirical data is now beginning to emerge related to domestic violence advocates and the influence of compassion fatigue on this profession (Mason, Wolf, O'Rinn, & Ene, 2017); Benuto, Yang, Ahrendt & Cummings, 2018). Ludick and Figley (2017), recommend a broader stroke with regards to much-needed research as it relates to professionals impacted by compassion fatigue and secondary traumatic stress, with victim advocates being considered noteworthy to this inclusion.

Negative Impact of Compassion Fatigue

The phenomenon of compassion fatigue has been trending (Kiley et al. 2018) due to the negative impact it places on the helper who is exposed to trauma, those they seek to support and the organizations where they serve. There is an emotional and physical toll placed on the helper for bearing witness to the trauma of clients. According to Koenig, Rodger, and Specht (2017), compassion fatigued helpers often exhibit symptoms along the spectrum of a diagnosis of post-traumatic stress disorder, to include elements of hyper-vigilance, forgetfulness, avoidance, and random flashbacks of the trauma shared by clients. Along with the manifestation of an unhealthy lifestyle (Nevins & Sherman, 2016) physiologically, helpers experience a myriad of biological challenges due to compassion fatigue, such as sleeplessness, depression, irritability and a compromised immune system with helpers even at-risk for a diagnosis of diabetes, increased heart problems and the development of alcohol use proclivities (Koenig, 2017; Andersen et al, 2015; Cetrano, 2017; Chiappo-West, 2017). In addition, to diminished physical capacities, helpers are subject to levels of emotional burnout (Pfaff et al, 2017)), by withdrawing from social support networks, developing relationship problems, suffering from guilt and the demonstration of self-harm ideations (Chiappo-West, 2017). Helpers often experience challenges in their social support networks, removing themselves from others experiencing relationship problems (Cetrano, 2017) and ultimately have poor coping skills in their own environment. According to Dutton, Dahlgren, Franco-Rahman, Martinez, Serrano & Mete (2017), those who provide therapeutic support and services to clients who have experienced trauma also suffer "cognitive effects—alterations in views about self, the world, and others that result from long-term empathic connection" (p.144).

Within organizations that house or employ helpers at risk of compassion fatigue, these agencies often experience a myriad of challenges with their helpers. Managers have expressed concern about compassion fatigue (Pfaff et al. 2017), amongst their workers

(Gerard, 2017; Kiley et al. 2018; Fisackerly et al. 2016), due to helpers having difficulty coping in their work environment, experiencing poor job satisfaction, and diminished levels of work productivity. Organizations must also deal with higher rates of absenteeism and requests to take sick leave increase (Pfaff et al, 2017), in addition to low morale, poor work communication (Chiappo-West, 2017), that impede service provision, costing organizations and the economy at large billions of dollars, in lost productivity every year (Gerard, 2017). In organizations attempt to create an empathetic and caring workforce, they have unintentionally created environments where their employees' needs are diminished in favor of the output of compassion to clients (Gerard, 2017) at the expense of their employees who are also in need of compassion.

The greatest disservice of compassion fatigue is on the one most deserving and in need of compassion - the client. In the literature review on compassion fatigue facilitated by Coetzee and Laschinger (2018), it was stated that compassion fatigue results in a detachment from clients, reduced empathy and the inability to provide intentional and compassionate service to clients, ultimately diminishing the organic capacity to demonstrate caring to clients. Fisackerly et al. (2016), indicates that workers internalize the challenges and trauma experienced by clients and this chronic exposure results in helpers no longer being able to bear the suffering of clients (Centrano, 2017). According to Alani & Stroink, (2015), those working in the field of domestic violence field are prone to experiencing the negative impact of working with such a traumatized population and even experience disdain and a lack of support from those in their inner circle and within the community (Dutton, Dahlgren, Franco-Rahman, Martinez, Serrano & Mete, 2017). To address these concerns, Houston-Kolnik et al. (2017), proffer that intentionality in self-care can aid in diminishing the adverse influence of this secondary traumatic experience. The following section will provide an overview of domestic violence, the advocacy work that helpers provide to victims and the resulting compassion fatigue they face.

Domestic Violence

Domestic violence is a phenomenon that is prevalent in society, having far-reaching implications for those who serve this population. Arroya, Lundahl, Butters, Vanderloo and Wood (2017) state that domestic violence is motivated by the desire to demonstrate control over a partner, which is facilitated by physical violence, emotional aggression and sexual assault by one partner to maintain power over the other partner. Whereas, another definition within the literature, posits that domestic violence includes behaviors such as physical aggression, sexual coercion, and psychological abuse physical, in turn producing the deleterious impact of physical, sexual, or psychological harm (Alvarez, Fedock, Grace & Campbell, 2017). The pervasiveness of domestic violence is far-reaching as Macy, Martin, Nwabuzor Ogbonnaya and Rizo (2018) report that annually there are 5 million occurrences of domestic violence which in turn, leaves an indelible impact on children and women (Postmus, Hoge, Breckenridge, Sharp-Jeffs, & Chung, 2018).

Domestic violence is a complex problem that has elements of this cycle manifest within society for centuries. According to Richard and Grover (2018), domestic violence once was considered a private issue that was confined within the walls of the family unit and now it has grown to be a complicated issue with grave societal implications. As reported by Grose and Grabe, S. (2014), considered a human rights violation domestic violence has global ramifications with 13- 61% of women worldwide experiencing physical violence, resulting in this phenomenon garnering close scrutiny across the international spectrums from educational institutions, advocacy groups and legislators alike. The National Coalition Against Domestic Violence reports that 1 in 3 women will experience intimate partner violence in their lifetime and over 15 million children a year are exposed to domestic violence. Sullivan and Virden (2017), highlight gender differences that women are more likely to be abused than men, resulting in devastating consequences running the gamut from deficiencies in mental health functioning to lifelong physiological challenges. Research on the subject of domestic violence has often focused on the physical abuse (Straus, 2017) and the external trappings of this problem (Postmus et al.;2018), whereas, Barocas, Emery and Mills (2016) states that the paradigm of domestic violence needs to be revisited to include a more expansive definition of this issue to include legalities, social services provision, research and policies that will improve outcomes for all involved in the cycle of abuse.

Domestic Violence Overview

The micro, macro and mezzo impact of domestic violence is concentric and comprehensive in nature, requiring closer examination, to fully understand the work of domestic violence advocacy. Domestic violence is a phenomenon that is prevalent in society, having far-reaching implications for those who serve this population. Wong and Bostwick (2017), simply define domestic violence as the emotional and/or physical abuse between family member or intimate partners whereas, Wijenayake, Graham & Christen (2018), provide more depth in definition, outlining abuse as intimidation by one partner in an intimate relationship, which can entail emotional abuse, physical abuse to include rape, and economic abuse, all aimed at demonstrating power and control by one partner over the other in a current or former relationship (Arroyo 2015). Macy, Martin, Nwabuzor Ogbonnaya and Rizo (2018), attest to domestic violence pervasiveness by reporting that annually there are 5 million occurrences of domestic violence within the United States, which in turn, leaves an indelible impact on families (Postmus, Hoge, Breckenridge, Sharp-Jeffs, & Chung, 2018). Research proffers that within the United States 1 in 3 women and 1 in 4 men have experienced a form of personal violation in their lifetime, ranging from physical violence, stalking and rape within an intimate partner relationship (Arroyo, 2017, Sullivan & Tyler, 2017).

Domestic violence is a complex problem that has had elements of this cycle manifest within society for centuries. According to Richard and Grover (2018), domestic violence was once considered a private issue that was confined within the walls of the family unit, and now it has emerged as a complicated issue with grave societal implications and numerous systemic causes (World Health Organization, 2012). One such explanation in the literature indicates that incarcerated prisoners were more likely to have experienced or witnessed domestic violence as a child and subsequently, perpetrate violence as adults (Will, Loper, Jackson, 2016) paving the way for intergenerational transmission of the domestic violence phenomenon. Research by Dargis and Koenigs (2017), also reveals that children who have observed domestic violence in childhood have poor coping skills and increased behavioral problems and may develop an adult proclivity to engage in domestic violence within intimate relationships (Green, Browne & Chou, 2017). Thus, the cycle of abuse (Richards, Tillyer & Wright, 2017) continues and is one element that contributes to the complex nature of domestic violence and the major social problem and public health dilemma of this issue. (Alvarez 2017; Arroyo, Lundahl, Butters, Vanderloo & Wood, 2017). Domestic violence can run the gamut of the spectrum of intimate partner controlling behaviors demonstrated physically, verbally, emotionally and financially along with many other controlling elements. Defining and addressing domestic violence is complex and broad in nature as researchers seek a greater understanding of coercive control and the means by which the perpetrator "forces physical, emotional, and financial dependency" (Postmus et al. 2018, p.2) on another. Barocas, Emery and Mills (2016) state that the paradigm of domestic violence needs to be revisited to include a more expansive definition of this issue to include legalities, social services provision, research and policies for outcomes to be improved for all involved in the cycle of abuse.

Researchers are seeking to carefully define this phenomenon, in addition to exploring the financial and health implications of domestic violence. The financial impact and cost of domestic violence in society is another overwhelming tenet of domestic violence that must be absorbed. Wijenayake Graham and Christen (2018), postulate the enormous cost of domestic violence on the general public and the National Coalition Against Domestic Violence (2018)concurs reporting that annually domestic violence costs in excess of 8 billion dollars. In literature facilitated by Murray, Crowe and Akers (2016), they reveal the financial implications of domestic violence due to the "high economic costs due to the healthcare, mental health care, legal services, survivors' basic needs, and economic consequences of lost productivity at work" (p.272). Specifically, short and long-term health care costs of domestic violence are overwhelming and the health implications staggering (Sprague et al. 2018; AlBuhairan, Abbas, El Sayed, Badri,

Alshahri & de Vries, 2017). The financial implication of domestic violence on society is expansive with research revealing services to victims one year after an abusive episode can result in costs upwards of 7 billion dollars, with healthcare costs comprising the most of this post-abuse financial output (Alvarez, 2017).

As other forms of abuse are often underreported, the most frequently researched dynamic of domestic violence is physical abuse as it is easily identifiable based on its external manifestation, (Macy et al. 2018, Postmus et al. 2018) and is often the focus of interventions. There is a clear distinction amongst types of abuse inflicted on victims and the intervention approach utilized to address it. Some stand-alone, while other elements merge and are juxtaposed. For the purpose of this study, the emphasis will be placed on advocates who work with clients who experience physical, sexual, emotional and financial abuse.

Physical Abuse: an intimate partner or family member may commit the act of domestic violence through the use of physical violence, by perpetrating bodily harm on the person they seek to control, resulting in pain with 75% of domestic violence incidences against women being physical in nature (Home Office, 2001). According to Shepard and Campbell (1992), physical abuse is utilized to augment and support all other types of abuse such as psychological abuse, which will rarely manifest without physical abuse. This type of abuse entails but is not all-inclusive to; *slapping, kicking, punching, pinching, choking, maiming, hair pulling, strangulation, and can result in death.*

Sexual abuse: According to the National Coalition Against Domestic Violence (NCADV) physically abusive partners are apt to also demonstrate sexually abusive behaviors towards their victims. This form of abuse can appear in several different ways, a complete act of sexual intercourse, attempted sexual abuse, contact sexually that inflicts pain and levels of uncomfortability related to sexual organs and sexual abuse contact in which the victim is forcibly exposed to unwanted sexual material or the use of verbal sexual language (domesticshelters.org, 2016). Heise (2018), reports that the majority of women who are sexually abused know their perpetrator. This type of abuse may entail; *forced sexual contact, forced sexual contact with people outside of the relationship, reproductive abuse, exposure to unwanted sexual material such as pornography.*

Emotional Abuse: This type of abuse is psychological in nature with the World Health Organization (2012), reporting that this type of abuse typically coexists with other abuse phenoms as the perpetrator seeks to inflict emotional distress. This type of abuse entails but is not all-inclusive to; *name-calling, silent treatment, blame, isolation, humiliation, intimidation, use of threats to abandon, to commit self-harm, threat of deportation, threat to take the children away, emotional blackmail (*Evans & Feder, 2016) *destruction of personal property.*

Financial Abuse: According to Postmus et al (2018), this type of abuse attempts to obtain control over the partner's finances and intervenes with accessibility to financial resources, causing a monetary hardship on household financial management. *This list of types of economic abuse is not exhaustive in nature but includes some of the following; the intentional destruction of independent financial credit, inappropriate use of funds, withholding financial support, acts of fraud using the partner's identity, the demonstration of negligent fiduciary responsibility.*

Domestic Violence Advocacy

With all that domestic violence entails, the support that is needed to assist domestic violence survivors is vast in nature. In research by Richards and Gover (2018), they share that victim advocacy manifested as an organizational and structural response to support required by domestic violence survivors, with a two-pronged tactic primarily geared toward client service provision and then a systemic approach to addressing, legislation, awareness and education related to domestic violence. According to Stover and Lent (2014), the role of the domestic violence advocate is vital in diminishing the intergenerational complexities and cycle of domestic violence from besieging future generations. To reconcile the trauma experienced, comprehensive services, supportive services and resources are often required to ameliorate survivor issues. Survivors often receive support and safety from local shelters, organizations proven to be beneficial (Arroyo et al. 2015) to survivors, that emerged as the Battered Woman's Movement in the 60's and 70's to provide survivors with wraparound services in a team decision-making capacity (Hackett, McWhirter & Lesher, 2016; Slattery & Goodman, 2017). The majority of research pertaining to domestic violence has placed focus on children and the impact of family violence on them, in addition to studies on batterer intervention strategies and treatment methodologies (Hackett, McWhirter & Lesher, 2016). The literature presents diverse practice modalities in the prevention and treatment of domestic violence that are broad in nature and scope, ranging from whole family intervention (Stanley & Humphreys, 2017), to web-based approaches (Tarzia et al. 2017), and traditional psychotherapeutic modalities for treatment (Barocas, Emery, Mills, 2016).

Domestic Violence Advocates

Central to the provision of domestic violence services is the advocate, who seeks to aid the survivor in navigating the circumference of the domestic violence systemic realm (Alani & Stroink, 2015; Macy et al, 2018; Barocas, Emery, Mills, 2016). Within the literature, whether they be known as domestic violence advocates (Evans, & Feder, 2016; Richards & Gover, 2018) or service providers (Macy et al. 2018; Alvarez et al. 2017) it is espoused that this work is manifest by an intrinsic motivation such as a "calling" (Wood, 2014) on their lives. Advocates are well rounded in service provision, serving collaboratively with providers (Richards & Gover, 2018) and providing comprehensive services to survivors from hotline crisis intervention, thorough assessments, housing support, counseling, legal advocacy, court accompaniment, the development of individualized treatment and safety plans and psychoeducational services (Frey et al. 2016; Macy et al. 2018). In their own way, each advocate is considered a frontline worker in the fight (Lehrner & Allen, 2009) against domestic violence. From the Executive Director of a community-based advocacy organization, serving as an advocate implementing strategies to obtain resources for victims, to the agency Court Advocate, who provides support to victims in legal matters, each serves as an advocate within their realm fulfilling their role to diminish the deleterious impact of domestic abuse (Lehrner & Allen, 2009). In the study on social change within the domestic violence movement, facilitated by Lehrner and Allen (2009), the majority of participants came from a domestic violence agency with study participants serving in advocacy roles ranging from "program coordinator, legal advocate, intake specialist, child advocate, counseling and advocacy, and executive director" (p. 659). Lehrner and Allen (2009) proffer that "domestic violence agencies are considered the backbone of the movement" (p.658) and based on this ideology justified the assorted aforementioned advocates participation in their research study on the movement of domestic violence advocacy. In addition, An and Choi, (2017) consider advocates frontline professionals, due to their unique skill set in advocacy, assessments and addressing victim service needs.

Just as domestic violence is a complex phenomenon (Barocas, Emery & Mills, 2016), the provision of services through advocacy, is also multi-dimensional and all-encompassing (Logan & Walker, 2018). Advocacy organizations have a vast responsibility to meet the complex and comprehensive needs of those victimized by domestic violence.

In research facilitated by Sullivan (2018), the Social and Emotional Wellbeing Framework highlights the conceptual model utilized to explore the efficacy and benefit of advocacy organizations. Domestic violence organizations are typically non-profit, and volunteer-based yet in spite of their framework they experience the pressure from local, state and federal legislative mandates to provide evidenced-based substantiation of their efficacy in helping this vulnerable population. Sullivan (2018) proffered that such organizations seek to ultimately promote survivor well-being through the lens of empowerment of self-efficacy and instilling a sense of hopefulness in survivors. This research punctuated that for most advocacy organizations the overarching goal is to diminish domestic violence and to ultimately promote individual and community well-being. According to Sullivan (2018), numerous studies have pointed out the benefit these organizations provide to the victim community. Yet there has been criticism of these studies based on shortcomings related to methodological structures such as the lack of comparative analysis and small sample size in these studies, subsequently, supporting the need for further research on the efficacy of advocacy in general. Nonetheless, Sullivan (2018), lauds the work of advocacy organizations for their short and long-term benefits to domestic violence survivors.

From a societal perspective, the infliction of physical abuse (Postmus, Hoge, Breckenridge, Sharp-Jeffs & Chung, 2018) on survivors obtains the most attention as it is a visual indicator of the abuse. Merchant and Whiting (2015), highlight the horror of physical abuse revealing that annually 9 million men and women, experience physical violence, relegated to being slapped, pushed and shoved which often results in the apex and finality of physical abuse, the death of the victim at the hands of an intimate partner. However, the trauma experienced by domestic abuse survivors is not typically relegated to one form of maltreatment, such as physical abuse (Straus, 2017), but it is most often intermingled and juxtaposed alongside other forms of abuse (Alvarez, Fedock, Grace & Campbell, 2017). A domestic violence survivor may experience financial and emotional abuse, whereas another survivor may be exposed to verbal and physical abuse.

As incidences of domestic violence do not operate singularly (World Health Organization, 2012), likewise, advocates do not work with victims based on a solitary or specific type of abuse the survivor may experience. Instead, domestic violence advocates implement a well-rounded and holistic approach to service provision (Kulkarni, Bell, Hartman and Herman-Smith, 2013, Richard and Grover, 2018, Evans & Feder, 2016). Advocates diligently work to address a multitude of systemic challenges survivors face from the abuse, such as their safety, housing, health and finances (Richard and Grover, 2018) and they do so in a multifarious manner linking survivors to appropriately delineated resources and services, based on the survivors individualized scenario and situation (Hughes, 2017). Domestic violence advocates provide these comprehensive services, all while addressing the most important and root cause of the cycle of abuse which stems from the power and control (Postmus, Hoge, Breckenridge, Sharp-Jeffs & Chung, 2018; Jones, 2016; Logan & Walker, 2018), inflicted upon the survivor, by the abuser. Shelters typically would house women and children in a safe place, providing emergency housing (Richard and Grover, 2018; Sullivan & Tyler, 2017) as a respite from the abuse and trauma inflicted upon them in their homes. In addition, these residential shelter facilities may provide or link survivors to clinical settings where psychotherapeutic services (Arroyo et al. 2015) are implemented along with support groups, financial advisory, medical support, housing assistance safety planning and comprehensive case management (Macy et al. 2018). While shelters seek to provide as much support as they can, these organizations are fraught with as many challenges as survivors may bring, as shelters may no longer fit in with survivor treatment modalities, do not have a home-like setting and give an institutionalized feel to what is supposed to be a home-like setting (Barocas, Emery, Mills, 2016; Aloni & Stroink, 2015). Domestic violence residents also reported additional negative components of living in shelters and findings in the literature indicate shelter life can either help or hinder survivor outcomes (Hughes, 2017; Arroyo et al. 2015).

The literature on domestic violence service provision touts the positive and rewarding components of working with families impacted by domestic violence through the phenomena of compassion satisfaction (Coetzee & Laschinger, 2018; Pfaff et al, 2017). In their study on domestic violence service providers Kulkarni, Bell, Hartman and Herman-Smith, (2013), sought to investigate the contributing factors of compassion satisfaction, secondary traumatic stress, which is often grouped as compassion fatigue (Sansbury, Graves & Scott, 2015, Killian, 2018) and burnout on domestic violence service providers. Exploring these elements from an organizational and individual perspective allowed researchers to ascertain how organizational worker mismatch may contribute to burnout and compassion fatigue. Through their web-based cross-sectional self-report survey of 236 respondents provided information pertaining to variables that included worker coping strategies, traumatic experiences, work environment factors, individual and organizational-wide risk and protective factors. Their findings revealed the importance of worker -organizational alignment of values and mission, self-perception and work experience, the use of self-care strategies as contributing factors in the achievement of compassion satisfaction.

In another study exploring the impact of working with trauma victims, Killian (2017), investigated the hurt workers may experience in their efforts to help others, espousing the challenges of helping when it hurts. In this study researchers point out a plethora of traumatic occurrences, to include the phenomenon of domestic violence that occurs within society that adversely impacts those who care for the traumatized. Their study had a dual focus, of which primary emphasis fell on the lived experience of professionals working with traumatized clients related to stress from their employment, measures for resiliency and finally an in-depth presentation of strategies for self-care. Secondarily, several variables such as self-awareness, work environment, worker trauma history and support network, were juxtaposed in relationship to compassion satisfaction, compassion fatigue and burnout were investigated. The literature review of this study presented data on the confluence of acute distress from exposure to ongoing exposure to client trauma and the resulting symptomology of post-traumatic stress disorder and disruption in the worker's worldview and capacity to function. The importance of coping strategies, education and awareness on this topic, were all highlighted within the literature. In addition, further training and worker immersion in leisure activities are recommended, to quell the impact of secondary trauma. The detriment of secondary trauma on domestic violence advocates is further supported in literature presented by Dutton, Dahlgren, Franco-Rahman, Martinez, Serrano and Mete (2017), wherein researchers found that 47.3% of domestic violence advocates who participated in a study related to compassion fatigue, endorsed clinical levels of posttraumatic symptoms, according to the Diagnostic and Statistical Manual of Mental Disorders.

Killian (2017), qualitative research included 20 licensed clinicians interviewed for the study based on their work with traumatized clients experiencing trauma. Uniquely the findings from this research produced hypotheses that were then utilized in a qualitative study with 104 workers specialized in working with the trauma population. Results revealed that having a solid support network contributed to compassion satisfaction, whereas, higher caseloads, more contact hours with traumatized clients can develop into compassion fatigue. No one strategy has been able to pinpoint a precise remedy to solve compassion fatigue and burnout syndromes. Due to the ongoing exposure to client domestic violence trauma, and the proclivity for advocates to experience secondary traumatic stress (Slattery & Goodman, 2017; Ludick & Figley, 2017) they must demonstrate a self-care regiment (Alani & Stroink, 2015) if they are to continue providing support to this vulnerable population.

Self-Care Strategies

Domestic violence advocates work with clients who are in crisis and this chronic exposure to trauma can result in this professional group being in need of self-care strategies to minimize the risk for compassion fatigue. Fisackerly (2016), reports that as a part of their employment and career responsibilities professionals engage with traumatized clients, and in return, these professionals may demonstrate elements of Post-Traumatic Stress Disorder, symptomology that mimic their client's trauma responses. To address this adverse result, research has strongly recommended participation in self-care measures to combat the adversity of exposure to trauma (Sansbury, Graves & Scott, 2015). In their qualitative study with women staff members at the YWCA, Brooks, Barclay and Hooker, (2018), it was recognized that workers experienced vicarious trauma from the chronic exposure to stories of violence and abuse. The literature also shared that as a result of vicarious trauma negative belief patterns would manifest ranging from hopelessness, helplessness or never being able to do enough, hypervigilance, chronic exhaustion and physical ailments, reduced ability to empathize, anxiety, cynicism, and overuse of substance (p.374). Out of this study, a multi-tiered approach to trauma-informed care manifested in an effort to combat vicarious trauma, ultimately espousing the implementation and importance of practitioners exercising self-care.

There is a plethora of literature on self-care strategies from within the nursing field (Mills, Wand, Fraser, 2015) which this phenomenon evolved. Defined within the literature, as the multidimensional approach to the intrinsic motivation and promotion of well-being and health in the prevention of external adverse influences (World Health Organization, 1998; Dorociak et al. 2017). Research has all but mandated as an ethical professional responsibility for workers to implement self-care practices as a means of providing stellar services and support to clients (Dorociak et al. 2017; Sansbury, Graves & Scott, 2015; Newell, Nelson-Gardell, & MacNeil, 2016, Nevins & Sherman, 2016). Self- care is individualized and encompassing a broad spectrum of activities that the professional would intentionally engage in to recharge, restore and be renewed (Kulkarni et al, 2013), in their efforts to provide care to those they seek to serve.

Research within the literature (Dorociak et al. 2017; Kulkarni et al. 2013), generally has self-care activities broken down into several quadrants to which all strategies fall within including exercise, nutrition, mindfulness, coping mechanisms, socialization systems and employer support and supervision;

Exercise: the incorporation of planned activities around achieving physical fitness is an important component of self-care. In addition to participation in leisure activities (Alani & Stroink, 2015), exercise, helps with body training and the increase in blood flow development of skeletal muscle mass. Those who engage in exercise have fewer risks associated with disease and illness and have an increase in body strength and stamina, less likely to fall into depression, as compared to those who are less active (World Health Organization, 2010)

Nutrition: eating poorly can significantly impact well-being (Corey, Muratori, Austin & Austin, 2017), and thus proper nutrition (Nevins & Sherman, 2016) in eating healthy foods helps to maintain physical prowess, which can help to augment mental fortitude and promise for future practices in professional care.

Coping Mechanisms – Those in professions exposed to compassion fatigue such as domestic violence advocate would need to deploy strategies to cope with the chronic trauma of clients. Such as meditation, mindfulness, prayer, relaxation, breathing techniques. Siegel (2017), as a burgeoning trend, mindfulness, touts the importance of being fully present without judgment to embrace the current situation. As a coping mechanism, professionals are utilizing this approach to holistically address self-care needs.

Support Systems – embracing meaningful relationships with friends and family can prevent isolation (Dorociak et al. 2017) that often manifest when self-care is not present. These informal networks help support and encourage workers and are beneficial to achieving self-care, serving as reminders about what is important and taking the focus off the trauma experienced in the professional setting.

Supervision –the literature punctuates the importance of supervision in the achievement of worker self-care strategies (Newell, Nelson-Gardell, & MacNeil, 2016; Alani & Stroink, 2015). When professionals, connect with trauma-exposed clients and feel supported by their organizations, and supervisors provide a genuine listening ear, with a platform for expression and transparency, it contributes to the self-care and well-being. In addition, the development and maintenance of positive relationships with cohorts can help to diminish the impact of secondary traumatic stress and help augment and solidify self-care (Dorociak et al. 2017).

There is a plethora of research on the relationship between burn out, compassion fatigue and the benefit of self-care strategies for helping professionals. In a qualitative study by Alani and Stroink (2015), they sought to gain a greater understanding of the thought process of female domestic violence workers and the self-care strategies utilized by female domestic violence advocates. Seven participants, all over the age of 25 provided cogent and detailed responses to the researcher's questions pertaining to lived experiences related to advocacy and self-care. Researchers progressively led participants in answering questions about safety planning, being the recipient of domestic violence client's trauma, challenges experienced in advocacy, individual and institutional barriers to self-care. Researchers were enlightened in knowing that some participants embraced doing additional work within this field related to awareness of domestic violence, was seen as a self-care strategy. Implications for future research highlighted the importance of including service providers in policymaking related to self-care implementation system-wide.

In studies emphasizing burn out, compassion fatigue and self-care in helping professionals, many researchers noted the dearth of research on this multi-pronged subject matter, specifically geared towards domestic violence advocates. Singer, Cummings, Boekankamp, Hisaka and Benuto, (2020), noted that the literature on this subject matter primarily featured helping professionals, such as social workers and largely excluded the unique work of victim advocates, and the impact of burnout and secondary traumatic stress on this particular helping profession. Likewise, it was noted by Benuto, Singer, Gonzalez, Newlands and Hooft, (2019) that focus is often placed on social workers and the impact of their work with trauma victims, and indicated that domestic violence victim advocates are another unique helping profession, that may be at-risk and in need of research to address negative byproducts of serving the traumatized. In addition, Globokar, Erez and Gregory, (2019), cite that extant literature has primarily focused on victim related issues and not on the manifold challenges faced by domestic violence victim advocates. It is in this vein that this research was being conducted to shed light on victim advocacy and the byproduct of compassion fatigue.

In addressing domestic violence advocates and compassion fatigue, the stance of the organizations they serve, play a vital role in augmenting or diminishing occupational risk factors. Kulkarni, Bell, Hartman and Herman-Smith (2013), reports that organizational structure can further heighten advocate issues with burnout and compassion fatigue due to poor agency support, minimal resources and lack of supervision. It has been reported that leaders within domestic violence advocacy organizations often demonstrated poor leadership with minimal awareness related to burn-out. even taking time off for self-care by advocates has been inconspicuously frowned upon by supervisors (Merchant & Whiting, 2015). Similarly, Powell-Williams, White and Powell-Williams (2013) chronicle the "minimization of worker distress, when it could be expressed in a constructive way" (p. 260) and that burnout threatens the ability for victim advocates to accomplish tasks that are set forth. Due to the many challenges faced by advocates who experience compassion fatigue, Cayir, Spencer, Billings, Hilfinger Messias, Robillard and Cunningham (2020) proffer that it is in the best interest of organizations to provide an environment that holistically fosters advocates well-being. As such, Benuto, Singer, Gonzalez, Newlands, and Hooft, (2019) concur with the role advocacy organizations play in providing support needed in mitigating occupational risk factors in the prevention of burnout and compassion fatigue.

The literature also espouses the benefits of self-care in addressing the complexities that stem from burnout and compassion fatigue in advocates. In research conducted by Killian (2008) it was indicated that there was no correlation between facilitating a certain type of self-care to reduce compassion fatigue. It is important to have a basic understanding of self-care in order to know what one's attitude is toward self-care practices (Nevin & Sherman, 2016) in order to diminish the impact of compassion fatigue. Considered one of the most important wellness actions that can be facilitated (Houston-Kolnik et al. 2017) as implementing self-care strategies within the helping field, are closely aligned with best practice outcomes for those being served (Alani & Stroink, 2015).

Methodology

This study utilized a qualitative descriptive study to determine the influence of self-care strategies domestic violence advocates utilize in the prevention of compassion fatigue. Vass, Rigby and Payne (2017), define qualitative studies based on the vast spectrum of ideologies and methodologies that can be extrapolated in understanding the perception and perspective of research participants. For this qualitative descriptive study, this research design draws from multiple data sources to glean information from domestic violence advocates in response to this study's research questions. The ultimate goal of a descriptive study lies within its name, as this approach seeks to describe a particular phenomenon while capturing the characteristics that lie therein (Nassaji, 2015). In addition, it also enables participants the ability to provide fluidity in their responsiveness without having to be confined by the specificity and rigidity of quantitative analysis. The multifarious dynamics of domestic violence advocacy, compassion fatigue and self-care juxtaposed are considered worthy of the exploratory investigation found in qualitative research, which would uncover great meaning in the advancement of scientific knowledge.

In particular, this researcher selected a descriptive methodological research design to ascertain the real-life experience of participants related to self-care strategies utilized by domestic violence advocates, in the prevention of compassion fatigue. It was anticipated that with this research design approach, rich and descriptive outcomes manifested from participants' responses based on the socio-cultural context from which they were expressed (Magilvy and Thomas, 2009). Research questions elicited from advocates on how self-care techniques were utilized within their sphere of professionalism and most importantly, uncover the connection and relationship (Baxter and Jack, 2008) between each of the study's elements. This research aligned with this study design, as qualitative descriptive studies are best utilized in exploring phenomena that are not truly understood (Kim, Sefcik & Bradway, 2017). Based on the aforementioned attributes of descriptive studies a determination was made that this approach was most suited to answer the research questions for this study.

Instrumentation

In examining the research question and qualitative approach, it was determined interviews and a focus group were deemed the most appropriate instrumentation to capture research data. While similar in their approach for using open-ended questions to elicit responses (Guest, Namey, Taylor, Eley and McKenna, 2017), each method has its own unique strength and approach in answering the research questions. According to Young et al (2018), interviews have been used for many years as a standard practice within social science research, and in a complementary fashion, focus groups can be buoyed based on the group dynamics and interactions (Guest, Namey, Taylor, Eley and McKenna, 2017).

This researcher proposes to facilitate interviews and a focus group with domestic violence advocates employed at a local domestic violence organization. The designated instrumentation is geared toward staff members and gaining an understanding of the influence self-care plays in the prevention of compassion fatigue for this professional group. All research participants will participate in this study by completing interviews or participating in a focus group. with this researcher capturing their responses (Potter & Hepburn, 2005) in open-ended questions, that will then be transcribed and eventually thematically analyzed.

This descriptive methodological research design was most suited for this study due to the real-life perspectives and responses that will be given in relation to the phenomenon (Flyvbjerg, 2006). In the research facilitated by Jones (2016), a qualitative approach was utilized on domestic violence advocates who self-identified as compassion fatigued. Similarly, to this research, the study sought to gain greater insight into the resilience of advocates in their innate ability to recognize compassion fatigue and apply this understanding to their self-care. The researcher utilized a generic qualitative inquiry research design to answer research questions, recognizing that this was not a study worthy of investigation in a quantitative laboratory setting environment. Data from within the research were extracted and coded for thematic analysis to provide research findings on this subject matter. Jones (2016), indicated that this methodology was chosen as best for the research design as generic qualitative inquiry provided the subjective, personal accounts and opinions of advocates in the self-identification of compassion fatigue.

For this current research study, interviews will serve as an instrumentation methodology, extracting an additional layer of data and perspective nuanced from the viewpoint provided in the focus group. It is anticipated that advocates will engage in the focus group answering questions in a semi-structured manner, which will also be captured and coded for data analysis. Researchers Guest, Namey, Taylor, Eley and McKenna (2017), have indicated that the interactive structure and informal nature of focus groups, often provide richer data than what single participants can produce. The methodology for this research will be qualitative in nature and utilize the instrumentation of interviews and focus groups to obtain data on self-care strategies from domestic violence advocates in the prevention of compassion fatigue.

Summary

Chapter 2 of this research study provided a comprehensive overview of the literature pertaining to this subject matter. Empirical data pertaining to compassion fatigue, domestic violence, advocacy and self-care were explored. These interrelated elements were thoroughly investigated to provide a greater understanding of the factors influencing this research. The gap within the literature pertaining to this research was exposed to determine the contribution this research would bring to the advancement of the body of knowledge. In addition, the theoretical framework was defined and examined in correlation to the research questions and methodological approach to distinguish its unique alignment to the study.

This literature review presented information on domestic violence and the billions of dollars spent in addressing this public health epidemic (Arroyo, Lundahl, Butters, Vanderloo & Wood, 2017). Domestic violence has a far-reaching impact on all facets of society. According to the National Coalition Against Domestic Violence, 2018 survivors experience significant trauma resulting from the power and control that abusers inflict.

The abuse endured by survivors is vast in nature, but includes, physical violence, emotional, verbal, sexual and financial abuse (Macy et al. 2018). Subsequently, Richards and Gover (2016), state that domestic violence advocates play an integral role in bringing about awareness and providing comprehensive services to survivors. As a component of their professional responsibility advocates is chronically exposed to the trauma (Benito, Yang, Ahrendt, & Cummings, 2018) of clients who often present to advocates in physiologically and psychologically distress. As advocates seek to ameliorate the issues survivors manifest with, they experience secondary trauma from the cost of caring (Pfaff, Freeman-Gibb, Patrick, DiBiase & Moretti, 2017), resulting in compassion fatigue (Butler, Carello, & Maguin, 2017, Fisackerly, Sira, Desai and McCammon, 2016). The phenomenon of compassion fatigue has a deleterious impact on domestic violence advocates the ability to provide noteworthy and beneficial services to this already traumatized population, impacting clients and the organizations they serve. Sorenson, Bolick, Wright, and Hamilton (2016) report in their research that empirical data has demonstrated that self-care strategies are effective to address compassion fatigue. However, there is a paucity of literature within the domestic violence realm to support this (Alani & Stroink, 2015), for domestic violence advocates. Subsequently, this research proposal seeks to answer the research question, regarding what are the most successful self-care techniques are used by domestic violence advocates in the Mid-Atlantic region of the United States, that help to prevent compassion fatigue and how do self-care techniques enable domestic violence advocates to prevent compassion fatigue?

The theoretical framework utilized to support and augment this research proposal is the Theory of Self-Care (Pfaff, Freeman-Gibb, Patrick, DiBiase & Moretti, 2017;

Orem, 1971). The construct of this theory was founded by Dorothea Orem in her quest to assist nurses to ward off the detriments of compassion fatigue. While this theory is typically found in the literature supporting medical research efforts, there has also been empirical data to support its use in the field of domestic violence (Campbell & Weber, 2000; Campbell, Kub, Belknap & Templin,1997) to address homeostasis. The theory embraces holistic functioning and the individual's innate ability and motivation in achieving self-care. The research methodology chosen to answer the research questions is a qualitative descriptive study, due to its ability to analyze information gathered from within the participant's context (Bowen, 2010), and its multimodal data collection measures. The particular instrumentations selected to facilitate this research are interviews and a focus group. These approaches were deemed to be the most optimal methodologies to answer the research questions, in an effort to add to the literature on this subject matter.

The subsequent chapter will fully encapsulate and highlight the methodology chosen to facilitate this research. Chapter 3 includes the selected research design to include empirical data to support its selection for this particular research. In addition, this chapter will elucidate the population chosen to research, the sample size and ethical considerations in conducting this study. This chapter will also explore the data collection and analysis procedures and the limitations, delimitations and assumptions made in the presentation of this research.

Chapter 3: Methodology

Introduction

The purpose of this qualitative descriptive study was to explore how domestic violence advocates who work with physically, mentally, sexually or financially abused clients in the Mid-Atlantic region of the United States, describe the influence of self-care in the prevention of compassion fatigue. This research study was explored through the theoretical framework of Orem's Theory of Self-Care. Domestic violence advocates are often secondarily exposed to the trauma that their clients witness (Benito, Yang, Ahrendt, & Cummings, 2018) and subsequently experience the negative after-effect of caring and supporting those who experience emotional abuse, psychological abuse, financial abuse and physical violence at the hands of a loved one (Macy et al. 2018). Within the field, this phenomenon has been coined as compassion fatigue, deemed a natural by-product (Killian, 2017) developed by professionals caring for those who are hurting. Literature reveals that self-care strategies are the most efficacious in diminishing the effects of compassion fatigue (Nelson, Hall, Anderson, Birtles & Hemming, 2018). However, it was not known the degree to which self-care strategies influence and diminish compassion fatigue in the lives of domestic violence advocates. Therefore, the gap in the literature this research sought to explore is the influence of self-care strategies on domestic violence advocates.

A qualitative descriptive study was the methodological approach utilized to answer the research questions of this study. In an effort to understand this phenomenon of self-care strategies within its context, a multi-modal data collection approach (Baxter & Jack, 2008) in the form of interviews and a focus group was determined to be most suitable. Subsequently, this chapter presents a comprehensive presentation on the manner in which this research was facilitated, with the following designated organizational outline; a statement of the research problem, examination of the research question, methodology and design, the population and sample to be utilized, instruments utilized to facilitate the research and the validity and reliability of these tools, data collection procedures and the manner in which data will be analyzed, ethical considerations and the limitations that may present within this study. To conclude this chapter, a summary of the aforementioned will be provided to fully encapsulate all the elements from within this methodological chapter.

Statement of the Problem

It is not known how self-care influences the prevention of compassion fatigue in domestic violence advocates who work with clients who are physically, mentally, sexually or financially abused. There is a substantial cost for caring (Pfaff, Freeman-Gibb, Patrick, DiBiase & Moretti, 2017) and many professions experience the deleterious effect of demonstrating continuous compassion to those who have been traumatized, which is characterized by Figley as a byproduct of working with clients who experience trauma ((Killian, 2017). Out of the field of psychology, researchers Pines and Maslach (Yip, Mak, Chio & Law, 2017), observed that the worldview of those who observed suffering, also suffered subsequently developing compassion fatigue. Those who serve in advocacy roles play an integral part in helping to stymie and bring awareness to this issue in an effort to quell the systemic ripple effect of this phenomenon, which costs billions of dollars per year (Arroyo, Lundahl, Butters, Vanderloo & Wood, 2017).

Domestic violence advocates are at times negatively impacted by their ongoing contact with trauma victims. The resulting cost of caring has been described in the literature by various names such as secondary traumatic stress disorder, vicarious trauma and compassion fatigue (Alani & Stroink, 2015; Sansbury et al. 2015; Benuto, Yang, Ahrendt, & Cummings, 2018; Hensel et al., 2015; Ludick & Figley, 2017)). Each of these conditions, while sharing the same systemic root causes, is different and has a negative impact on the professional from depression, absenteeism, lack of empathy and disengagement from services (Koenig, 2017; Andersen et al, 2015; Cetrano, 2017; Chiappo-West, 2017). Domestic violence advocates are not immune from experiencing compassion fatigue based on their line of work bearing witness to acute and chronic trauma.

Power and control issues demonstrated by perpetrators are at the root of domestic violence episodes (Postmus, Hoge, Breckenridge, Sharp-Jeffs & Chung, 2018), which often manifest through emotional, financial, psychological and physical abuse (Evans & Feder, 2016). In a quest for safety and amelioration of abuse issues, survivors often seek refuge within domestic violence organizations ((Richard and Grover, 2018; Sullivan & Tyler, 2017). Within these organizations and support systems, as part of their professional responsibilities, domestic violence advocates are regularly exposed to the trauma their clients have endured. Chronic exposure to trauma by professionals can manifest in deleterious outcomes for the professional (Hensel, Ruiz, Finney & Dewa, 2015), which can impede their ability to function optimally and in the best interest of the client.

Research has indicated that in order to efficaciously combat the ills of compassion fatigue, self-care strategies should be deployed to remedy the effects of constant exposure to trauma. A review of the literature did not present research facilitated on the degree to which self-care strategies influence domestic violence advocates in diminishing the harmful effects of compassion fatigue. Subsequently, this research produced research questions surrounding the influence of self-care in compassion fatigue prevention to which this researcher sought to gain answers for each research question.

Sources of Data

In this qualitative descriptive study, there will be two sources of data that will be utilized to answer the research question on the influence of self-care in the prevention of compassion fatigue. The sources of data that will be utilized to understand this phenomenon were interviews and a focus group. Whitehead and Baldry (2018) state that interviews and focus groups have long held a dominant place in social science qualitative research as these sources of data can provide significant insight into the phenomenon being explored. Interviews and a focus group will answer the research questions and generate findings that can elucidate the subject matter and add to the body of knowledge related to this research topic.

Interviews

Participants that engage in the interview portion of this research will participate in a semi-structured interview process in order to answer research questions related to self-care strategies and how this protocol diminishes the influence of compassion fatigue. In order to facilitate the interviews in a manner convenient for participants, several interview options will be presented in which they may select the method most appropriate for their schedule. Interview options such as face to face, videoconference or telephonic participation will be made available based on participant preference. Face to face interviews may be conducted at the organization or in a location convenient to the participant. In addition, video conference mechanisms such as Skype, Zoom Meetings or GoToMeetings can be a convenient mechanism to conduct interviews. Considered a new methodological frontier, video conference abilities are changing the landscape of social science research data collection in the analysis of human behavior, particularly with the increase in digital communication (LeBaron, Jarzabkowski, Pratt & Fetzer, 2018; Weller, 2017).

Participants may also have the accessibility and capacity to utilize the telephone as a means to conduct the research interview. However, in offering this approach this researcher must be aware of certain nuances as James (2016), reports that with telephonic interview usage there may be challenges with data interpretation due to the lack of visual context from which to comprehend participant responses. Due to the small sample population from which to obtain participants, this researcher does not want to exclude any options by which participants may avail themselves to participate in interviews. However, this researcher will utilize this telephonic approach if it is the only means by which a participant can make themselves available for this study. To ensure systematic uniformity throughout each interview it is beneficial to develop and utilize an interview guide (Goodell, Stage & Cooke, 2016) to serve as a script and protocol (Appendix E) to adhere to in the facilitation of the interviews.

Interviews will be semi-structured to include all open-ended questions, which will allow room for the interviewer to further probe responses and interviewees to provide clarification of their answers. At least 60 minutes will be allotted for each interview to take place which should be sufficient time for participants to share their lived experiences and insights related to self-care strategies and compassion fatigue. Each participant will be asked qualifying information to determine their eligibility to participate in the research, upon thorough vetting, participants will be permitted to proceed in the remainder of the interview study. Interview questions will commence with reflective questions based on the influence of self-care strategies in the prevention of compassion fatigue. The interview portion of this study will seek to answer this study's research questions, in order to ascertain the influence typically utilized self-care strategies have on domestic violence advocates in the Mid-Atlantic region of the United States, who work with clients who are physically, mentally, sexually or financially abused, in preventing compassion fatigue.

Focus Group

To further augment the data collected from the interviews completed by domestic violence advocates who work in a family violence center in the Mid-Atlantic region of the United States, additional participants will engage in a focus group facilitated by this researcher. Emphasis will be placed on this target population answering research questions related to the influence of self-care strategies in the prevention of compassion fatigue. This data source was determined most optimal as Guest, Namey, Taylor, Eley and McKenna (2017), indicate group dynamics can produce stimulating dialogue and generate data that may not readily be obtained from extant sources. The focus group will take place at a designated location within the agency, in order to ensure convenience and accessibility for participants. The time allotted for the focus group will be two (2) hours to ensure that there is sufficient time for all focus group participants to share information related to self-care in the prevention of compassion fatigue.

This researcher will utilize an interview/focus group guide (Goodell, Stage & Cooke, 2016), as a checklist to ensure all elements of the focus groups are followed to ensure uniformity (Appendix I). This researcher will serve as a moderator for the focus group, enabling participants the liberty to disclose, dialogue and contemplate the influence of self-care in the prevention of compassion fatigue. The focus group portion of this study will seek to answer both research questions pertaining to the influence of self-care in the prevention of compassion fatigue within the domestic violence sample population.

Expert Panel Validation and Field Testing

To ensure that questions asked in interviews and the focus group met projected outcomes, these questions were reviewed, assessed and vetted by professionals within the field of research. This researcher convened an expert panel, considered stakeholders within this particular field of research, they were besought for their ability to synthesize and provide sound recommendations pertaining to the subject matter (Waltz et al, 2015) this approach was also considered an exemplary research strategy (Manzano, 2016). This researcher convened expert panelists to review the questions that were asked of each participant in the interview and focus group portion of this study. Fusch & Ness (2015), concurred that this process provided an additional layer of data saturation and diminishes researcher bias. By their thorough review and vetting of research questions, members of the expert panel were able to validate that the questions being asked of participants would indeed answer the research questions this researcher had compiled.

For this research, initial interview and focus group questions were sent to seven (7) doctoral expert professionals via email (Appendix G) of which three (3) consented to participate as expert panelists for this research study. All three (3) had terminal doctoral degrees and significant knowledge as either qualitative researchers or subject matter expert professionals. In order to ensure consistency in the review of interview and focus group questions amongst panelists, the Validation Rubric for Expert Panel (White & Simon, 2019) was utilized. Permission to utilize this validation tool was granted by Marilyn Simon via email correspondence (Appendix E & F). This tool provided criteria upon which panelists scored interview questions, assessing the use of jargon, wordiness, bias and whether or not questions have the necessary structure needed to answer the over-arching research question. Consenting Expert Panelists were emailed and provided the VREP along with the interview/focus group questions (Appendix H) and upon completion, they emailed the VREP to this researcher (Appendix I) with their respective feedback.

Expert panelists strongly recommended that the constructs of terminology such as compassion fatigue and self-care be operationalized, and a greater understanding of these terms needed to be asked of participants. By proffering the question in this manner, it would prevent less ambiguity and generate the focus and specificity participants needed in order to answer questions comprehensively and provide depth in response to what this researcher was seeking. Expert panelists' feedback was incorporated in the compilation of a revised (Appendix I) version of research questions, that appeared significantly more cohesive and provided the depths needed to answer this study's overall research question.

Expert panelists provided noteworthy feedback that was addressed by this researcher with recommended changes incorporated in questions for interviews and the focus group.

In addition to research data instruments being reviewed by expert panelists, these questions were also vetted and solidified by field testers. This practice of testing out questions that would be asked of the sample population helped to ensure the responses would ultimately meet the targeted objective of the designated research questions. Interview and focus group questions were comprehensively vetted by those within the field, providing the opportunity for those within the profession but not part of the sample population to test the efficacy of each question being asked of participants. This researcher conducted field test interviews with several people in the field of domestic violence advocacy to practice focus group and interview questions, these interviews lasted between 20 – 30 minutes. After each field test all three (3) interviews were transcribed and resulted in nine (9), ten (10) and thirteen (13) pages. To ensure this research yields sufficient data, follow-up questions enable participants to elaborate on responses provided to help to ensure there is ample data captured for thematic analysis. Those designated to participate in field testing were informed that they would not participate in the formal research study.

Although four to five (4-5) domestic violence advocates were requested to participate in field testing, this researcher obtained three (3) participants to conduct interviews via teleconference. Domestic violence field testers provided salient feedback on the questions that were asked of them pertaining to the influence of self-care in the prevention of compassion fatigue. It was indicated that some questions appeared redundant and respondents felt as though they had answered certain questions previously.

Research questions did provide the appearance of being redundant due to similar questions being asked related to compassion fatigue and then pertaining to self-care strategies. Participants did seek clarification on the definition of terminology utilized such as compassion fatigue and the meaning of self-care. Once it was ascertained that this researcher and participants were on the same page pertaining to these terms, they were able to answer research questions with ease. The flow of the practice field testing yielded positive results and experience for participants who were eager to share their experiences related to this subject matter and its influence upon their profession. The process of field-testing research questions was beneficial in providing a medium in which this researcher practiced and had a pre-experiential opportunity prior to conducting legitimate questioning for this research.

Research Questions

This qualitative descriptive study sought to explore the influence of self-care on domestic violence advocates, in the prevention of compassion fatigue. A descriptive research design was used when seeking to understand a phenomenon in its individualized context (Baxter & Jack, 2008). This design approach was considered best suited to support research studies that sought to be descriptive in nature (Colorafi & Evans, 2016) as this research provided descriptions of self-care from domestic violence advocates. This research design was selected in order to explore the influence of self-care strategies in the prevention of compassion fatigue in domestic violence advocates.

Domestic violence advocates were the focus of this study serving as the target population for this qualitative descriptive study. It was projected that 25-30 domestic violence advocates in the Mid-Atlantic region of the United States would participate in interviews and a focus group. Domestic violence advocates would volunteer to answer research questions pertaining to self-care strategies utilized in the prevention of compassion fatigue. The responses to the research questions would be derived from domestic violence advocates from the Mid-Atlantic region of the United States, serving as the target population for this research. Participants for this study would be domestic violence advocates who provide comprehensive domestic violence services from a family violence organization.

For this qualitative descriptive study, there were two different groups extracted from the larger target population, wherein it was anticipated that twenty-five to thirty (25-30) advocates would participate to answer research questions. With attrition in consideration, it was estimated that twelve to fifteen (12-15) advocates would participate in interviews, and six to eight (6-8) participants would participate in the focus group. Those who participated in interviews would not have the opportunity to participate in the focus group and likewise, those selected for the focus group would not participate in interviews. Subsequently, each group within this population would be asked the same questions in fulfillment of answering the overarching research questions designated for this study.

The research questions for this study are as follows;

RQ1: What self-care techniques do domestic violence advocates from the Mid-Atlantic region of the United States describe as typically being used in the prevention of compassion fatigue?

RQ2: How do domestic violence advocates from the Mid-Atlantic region of the United States use self-care to prevent compassion fatigue?

Research question one provided the foundation for this study in engaging participants in dialogue as it pertains to self-care strategies and compassion fatigue. This question provided the gateway response for the various types of self-care strategies that domestic violence advocates utilize. In addition, it would elucidate which self-care strategies were typically utilized and deemed most beneficial in the prevention of compassion fatigue. Research question two expounds upon the capacity in which self-care supports the prevention of compassion fatigue. While research indicates that self-care is vital to the prevention of compassion fatigue (Dorociak, Rupert, Bryant & Zahniser (2017), it would add to the body of empirical data to explore the magnitude to which self-care strategies genuinely influence the prevention of compassion fatigue within this population. As a research tool, twelve-fifteen interviews would be conducted with six-eight domestic violence advocates participating in a focus group, in order to ascertain the magnitude of the influence to which self-care strategies are effective in diminishing compassion fatigue within this sample population.

Research Methodology

A qualitative approach was deemed to be the most viable methodology to answer this study's designated research questions. In an effort to gain greater understanding regarding the influence of self-care strategies in the prevention of compassion fatigue, research was conducted with this population within the context of their environment in order to obtain their lived experiences and processes related to this phenomenon. With its emphasis on meaning, interpretation (Gough & Lyons, 2016;) and the multimodal data sources qualitative research provided the explorative foundation needed to answer the gap within literature for this study, as opposed to other research methodologies with

Gough and Lyons, (2016) reporting that qualitative research supports the effectual development of psychological knowledge.

In particular, qualitative research was chosen for this study as it allowed for thematic analysis (Gough & Lyons, 2016), based on responses from participants to determine whether there are any patterns and similarities (Baxter & Jack, 2008). This research seeks to uncover which self-care strategies are most widely used by this sample population based on their individualized and unique perspectives. Therefore, analyzing and making a determination regarding thematic patterns as afforded in qualitative research would be most beneficial to this study, as responses from domestic violence advocates regarding this subject matter appear tacit within empirical data. Levitt, Bamberg et al., (2018) affirm this statement and methodological choice stating that qualitative research "gives a voice to historically disenfranchised populations whose experiences may not be well-represented in the research literature" (p.28).

For the purpose of this research, a quantitative approach was deselected as a methodology, in favor of a more suitable qualitative design. The generalized purpose of quantitative research is to obtain a measurement of variables in quantifiable terms that undergo statistical analysis with information typically obtained from predetermined tools such as questionnaires and surveys (Young et al (2018). Subsequently, this approach can lack the depth of understanding that can only be obtained from a qualitative methodology (Mertler, 2018; Boeren, 2018). In addition, this research did not seek to understand the correlations or measurement between self-care strategies but to elucidate the various types of self-care strategies, in particular, to establish a baseline of the most successfully used strategies as practiced by domestic violence advocates.

This qualitative approach was further supported in empirical articles that were similar to this research on domestic violence advocates. In their research on self-care and domestic violence Alani and Stroink (2016), used a qualitative methodology to expound on the thoughts of advocates related to self-care and barriers to achieving self-care. In another research study on domestic violence advocates and their ability to manage their emotions when working with domestic violence victims, Powell-Williams, White and Powell-Williams (2013), used a qualitative approach in answering research questions on occupational stress. In another similar study, Houston-Kolnik, Odahl-Ruan and Greeson (2017) used a qualitative approach in their research with rape victim advocates as they explored social supports to address secondary traumatic stress. Jones (2016) research also used a qualitative approach in exploring how victim advocates self-identified as compassion fatigue. Each of these qualitative studies was similar to this study and justified why this methodology was most optimal and selected as opposed to quantitative research methods.

A qualitative approach is most appropriate as the various research designs provide numerous data methods (Boeren, 2018), from which to select from as a foundation from which to extrapolate the information needed for this research. According to Baskarada (2014), the variety of tools utilized in qualitative research enables the researcher to collect and examine data through multiple lenses. This researcher was able to explore and examine the subject matter with the fluidity that qualitative research affords without the regimented and structured approach frequently found in quantitative studies.

To further justify the use of qualitative methods for this study is the small sample size selected that are typically used in this approach, as opposed to quantitative methods wherein voluminous data (Malterud, Siersma, & Guassora, 2016) can be statistically analyzed. In addition, a modicum of sample sizes enables the researcher to become fully immersed with participants to gain the comprehensiveness that is required to understand the complexity in diminishing compassion fatigue through the use of self-care strategies within this population. Quantitative research typically seeks to hypothesize outcomes with predetermined variables and correlations, whereas, with a qualitative approach this researcher is unencumbered by fixed and measured parameters. The most influential component in the selection of qualitative research methodology for this study is the ability to obtain incremental responses to provide a contextual understanding of the phenomenon (Bowen, 2010).

Research Design

For this research study, a qualitative descriptive research design was selected in order to answer the research question pertaining to the influence of self-care strategies in the prevention of compassion fatigue for domestic violence advocates. Colorafi and Evans (2016) support the use of a descriptive research design for the naturalistic foundation that it provides and that it supports "factual responses to questions about how people feel about a particular space… and the factors that facilitate or hinder use" (p.17). The elements of this design are supported in this research that will be exploring the influence of self-care and factors that prevent compassion fatigue. Descriptive research designs provide an organic environment in which to obtain participants' responses therefore, utilizing a descriptive research design provides the gateway in which to whittle down the research matter to extrapolate further understanding and keen insights from research participants.

With a plethora of research opportunities to select from, such as interviews, focus groups and direct observations, it enables the researcher to examine and extrapolate participants' personal experience within an organic environment. This design methodology is deemed the worthiest to enhance the credibility of information collected as this approach uses multiple sources to collect data (Baxter & Jack, 2008) allowing the researcher the ability to submerge in the multimodal data collection opportunities this approach affords. This research design approach was affirmed by Nassaji (2015), indicating that a descriptive research design provides further depth in the understanding of meaning without the need for external manipulation of data. Within the body of this research, a descriptive study provided the outlet from which advocates shared their perspective.

Other research designs were not selected for this research study as they did not meet the best criteria in which to answer research questions. Research designs such as a correlational approach would not be appropriate for this study as there are no variables or hypotheses to contrast, examine or pit against each other (Turner, Cardinal & Burton, 2017) in exploring the influence of self-care in the prevention of compassion fatigue. A narrative approach was not selected as this research did not seek to obtain the in-depth stories of participants (Creswell, Hanson, Clark Plano & Morales, 2007) and their self-care, nor chronologically re-tell participants story as it relates to this subject matter. In addition, this descriptive study design seeks to uncover the natural phenomena as expressed by advocates related to their self-care (Zainal, 2017) in contrast the construct of a narrative approach would provide a more global interpretation of events (Dalpiaz &

Di Stefano, 2017) instead of a more specific approach being sought in this particular research.

Several other research designs such as case studies, phenomenology and a grounded approach were deemed not suitable for this study. A Case Study was not selected for this research as the tendency with this approach is to become overly engrossed in examining data and broad concepts (Baxter & Jack, 2008), wherein this study seeks to have a descriptive overview in understanding the phenomenon of self-care in the prevention of compassion fatigue in this population. A phenomenological design was not chosen for this study as there was no need for this researcher to be immersed within the social setting of this population to obtain a first-hand account and lived experience of the target sample population (Nag, Snowling & Asfaha, 2016; Flasch, Murray & Crowe, 2017). A grounded theory research design was not selected for this research as there was no need to capture a theory grounded in the data obtained (Ruppel & Mey, 2015), as the purpose for this study was to describe the influence of self-care in the prevention of compassion fatigue and not to develop or manifest a theoretical framework based on the data captured.

Unit of Analysis & Unit of Observation

In exploring the influence self-care on domestic violence advocates in the prevention of compassion fatigue, this study will encompass units of analysis and unit observation. The unit of analysis is typically determined by the problem statement of the research study and is highlighted by the unit that is being observed (Blackstone, 2012). This study's unit of observation are individual Domestic Violence Advocates, facilitated by interviews and a focus group with domestic violence advocates to include member checks of the data collected. Subsequently, the data that will be collected from interviews will be on the individual level of domestic violence advocates. The second data source utilized was a focus group and subsequently, the unit of observation for this data source were individual domestic violence advocates who served as the target population for this study.

Data Collection. It is the wide-ranging data collection tools utilized in descriptive studies that made this approach the most suitable for this research. Being able to obtain data from multiple angles provided an eclectic and unique context from which to analyze and understand the designated research. To add their contribution to the body of knowledge, a specific approach was utilized to extrapolate the necessary data, patterns, and themes from participants. Subsequently, interviews and a focus group were strategically selected as data tools for this study with domestic violence advocates.

To collect the necessary data to answer the research questions, it was recommended that interviews would be conducted with domestic violence advocates from the same organization. According to Young et al (2018), interviews have been used for many years as a standard practice within social science research as an interactive process in which the interviewer and interviewee learn from each other in the development of the presented research information in a one on one environment. In addition, interviews allow the researcher the ability to ask probing questions to gain a greater understanding of participant responses, an approach that could not be achieved if a more stringent research design had been selected. To further support the use of interviews, for his research design, Alani and Stroink (2015) and Jones (2016), used interviews in their studies with domestic violence advocates in order to gain a greater understanding of their thoughts and feelings in working with this population in relation to their self-care. Interviews conducted with domestic violence advocates would present open-ended questions in order to foster a dialogue to elicit information on self-care strategies utilized by participants in the prevention of compassion fatigue.

To further augment and collect the necessary data to answer the research questions, a focus group would be coordinated consisting of domestic violence advocates. According to O Nyumba, Wilson, Derrick, & Mukherjee (2018), progressively, there has been an increase in focus groups across research disciplines based on its participatory nature and the ability for the researcher to serve as moderator in the facilitation of participant discussion pertaining to the subject matter. Research has indicated that the interactive structure and informal nature of focus groups often provide richer data than what single participants can produce (Guest, Namey, Taylor, Eley & McKenna, (2017). In their study Brooks, Barclay and Hooker, (2018) utilized a focus group with workers exposed to violence and found the benefit of open-ended questions provided in focus groups encouraged participants to be more open in sharing their respective stories. In addition, focus groups work complimentarily and cohesively with other data collection sources (Young et al (2018), as will be the case in pairing the focus group with interviews from this study.

In contrast, questionnaires were de-selected from this data collection process due to a myriad of factors specifically related to close-ended questions, lack of clarification and ambiguity in response. According to Krosnick (2018), questionnaires often include close-ended questions and research has indicated that these responses can significantly decrease reliability. In addition, respondents are unable to obtain clarification they may have on questionnaire queries and can easily respond with "don't know "(Krosnick, pg.283) due to ambiguity related to the research question. In contrast, interviews and focus groups share similar open-ended question techniques to elicit responses, yet they are not synchronous in approach, as each method has their own unique strength and approach in answering research questions.

Population and Sample Selection

The population of interest to which the results of this study would be applicable are domestic violence advocates in the Mid-Atlantic region of the United States. The anticipated target population for this study are domestic violence advocates in the Mid-Atlantic region of the United States who work at a family violence organization, of which the study sample will be drawn from. In order to answer research questions on the influence of self-care on domestic violence advocates in the prevention of compassion fatigue, domestic violence advocates who reside in the Mid-Atlantic region of the United States will serve as the target population for this study. It is estimated that 25-30 domestic violence advocates who work in a Family Violence Center, will serve as the sample population in providing the final source of data. A descriptive research design will be utilized for this study with 12- 15 participating in interviews and 6-8 in a focus group.

Research purports that within the scope of interviews, the sample size is not considered as vitally imperative as the information gleaned for analysis (Malterud, Siersma, & Guassora, 2016) and according to O Nyumba, Wilson, Derrick, & Mukherjee (2018), it is acceptable to have a sample size of six to eight (6-8) participants for focus groups. At a minimum, focus groups should include six to twelve (6-12) participants, large enough to ensure diversity of thought and small enough in size to foster comfortability for participants to communicate (Fusch & Ness, 2015). Sample participants must be over the age of eighteen (18) years old, be employed at a local domestic violence organization in the Mid-Atlantic region of the United States and serve as a domestic violence advocate for over a year and provide informed consent (Appendix C) to participate in the research. While the target population for this research were all considered domestic violence advocates, participants may have assorted functions (Benuto, Yang, Ahrendt, & Cummings, 2018; Richards & Gover, 2016), and titles, such as hotline workers, shelter case managers, child therapists and court advocates. Despite their roles being different, they all work on the front lines in their respective roles as domestic violence advocates, doing their part to cohesively mitigate, the ramifications of domestic violence. Participants for this study will be asked what their domestic violence advocate role is at the onset of the interview and focus group.

In order for this research study to be conducted permission must be granted by the organization to facilitate research at their agency with their employees and volunteers. An email has been submitted to the Executive Director (Appendix D) requesting site authorization and it has been signed and returned to this researcher granting approval (Appendix A). Once Institutional Review Board authorization (Appendix B) is granted, the recruitment of sample participants will commence, wherein this researcher will request that executive leadership submit a letter or email to employed staff members of the organization. It will be requested that those domestic violence advocates who are interested in participating in this research contact this researcher, via email or telephone to indicate their interest in participating in this study.

For this research, purposive sampling will be utilized to obtain participants, due to the ease of accessibility to participants for this research. Purposive sampling is known as a type of selection process where members of the target population meet certain practical criteria (Etikan, Musa & Alkassim, 2016). Once advocates make contact with this researcher an overview of confidentiality expectations and guidelines will be presented to participants, to ensure all human subjects are protected (Kue, Szalacha, Happ, Crisp & Menon, 2018) in this research, and given assurances that what is disclosed will remain confidential. Each participant comprehensively had explained to them the confidentiality policies of this research, in addition to a request made for each participant to sign an Informed Consent (Appendix C).

This researcher would continue to engage the organization in recruitment with the hopes of obtaining sufficient participants. In the event that there are insufficient volunteers for the study from the original organization, another family violence organization within the Mid-Atlantic region will be contacted to seek permission to recruit domestic violence advocates for this study. This recruitment process will continue until this researcher has sufficient participants to satisfy sample size criteria. The target population and sample size for this study have been vetted to ensure they fall within the normative standards for this type of qualitative descriptive study research design. The following section elaborates on the sources of data utilized for this study.

Ethical Considerations

In the process of facilitating research and obtaining information from human subjects, it was vitally important that their contribution and privacy was secure and protected. It was the ethical obligation of this researcher to ensure that the confidentiality of all participants was adhered too, in order to minimize the risk of disclosure and violation of participant privacy (Wolf, Patel, Tarver, Austin, Dame & Beskow, 2015). Prior to research being facilitated permission from the Institutional Review Board was obtained and all research protocols followed. Human subjects were utilized for this study and informed consent was secured from participants and the organization in which they were employed prior to research participation. Letters were sent to organization leadership outlining the scope of the research to be conducted and seeking site authorization. Upon approval, to prevent disclosure of participant identity, every subject will be given a unique identifier code with all data collected, securely placed in two different locations for a period of 4-5 years as ascribed by federal guidelines and mandates. Data collected were secured on two password-protected thumb drives and kept in separate locations. This researcher included a declaration statement indicating there were no conflicts of interest or maladaptive ethical issues on the part of the researcher in the facilitation of this research.

In addition, ethical issues related to working with such a fragile population were taken into consideration to ensure that participating in this research would or would not exacerbate symptoms of compassion fatigue. Utmost care was taken to ensure domestic violence survivors working with staff members were not informed about the research as they may have attempted to utilize this information related to self-care and compassion fatigue as rationale for perceived poor service, limited access to resources and a diminished perception of the professional expertise of domestic violence advocates in the provision of therapeutic services.

This researcher ensured that the dignity of participants was respected by securing their privacy, and any information obtained through the course of interviews and the focus group was well-regarded and not shared with other participants. In addition, the benefits and harm of participating in this research were discussed and explored with all participants. An ethical issue considered related to participants in the focus group having a pre-existing relationship, and the influence this would have upon disclosure and active participation in the focus group. While it was recommended that focus group participants should not be known to each other (Sim & Waterfield, 2019), participants in this study all worked together in the same organization. In order to address ethical issues that manifested from pre-existing coworker relationships of focus group participants, this researcher reiterated the importance of confidentiality and not repeating what is shared beyond the confines of the focus group to include a reminder, related to non-disclosures.

Trustworthiness

Within the realm of qualitative research, trustworthiness is established and deemed necessary in order to highlight the virtue and verity of the designated study. Trustworthiness within this descriptive research design was upheld, augmented and supported through the collaboration and manifestation of credibility, transferability, dependability and confirmability (Gunawan, 2015). Each of these elements interfaced with the other and played a distinct role in the development of the trustworthiness required to validate this study.

Credibility

Within the field of qualitative research ensuring a study has credibility is one of the most important (Connelly, 2016) and viable criteria in the establishment of trustworthiness. The development and necessity for reliability and trustworthiness within research methods manifested primarily to examine rigor within quantitative studies, however, according to Maher, Hadfield, Hutchings and de Eyto (2018), it also remains apropos for qualitative endeavors, and can be considered challenging to accomplish within the context of this research design. Credibility is also facilitated through a systemic practice that is implemented to ensure engagement, durability and oversight within the research process (Korstjens & Moser, 2018). Credibility manifested in through the means of assorted data sources and member checking.

Data Sources is the use of assorted data source mechanisms to answer research questions and when each data source generates the same outcome then credibility can be achieved (Cutcliffe & McKenna,1999). For this study a dual pronged approach was utilized in the form of interviews and a focus group. It was anticipated that participants would engage in interviews where they would share information related to the influence of self-care in the prevention of compassion fatigue. In addition, the focus group was held where participants answered research questions. While each data capturing mechanism was different it was considered appropriate to utilize these approaches to augment and solidify the practice of credibility. Data collected from interviews and the focus group was then analyzed and the same themes manifested in the answer to research questions. For this research study, data was collected from interviews and a focus group to capture different dimensions of the phenomena of this study. For this research, the first implementation of data collection would be through the use of interviews, and a focus group added to the quality and richness of data collected at a different time.

Member checking is another means by which this researcher established credibility. Smith and McGannon (2018), affirm the utilization of member checking, where the transcribed interviews and a summary of the interview, would be returned to participants for their review to ensure accuracy and that the intent of what was expressed was accurately captured without bias from the researcher. This comprehensive review provides the authentication needed to ensure the credibility of what was communicated in each interview and focus group. For the purpose of this study, shortly after the conclusion of data collection via interviews and focus group, this researcher obtained the transcribed data and returned it to participants via email for their review. Each participant was given seven (7) days to examine the information shared in the interview or focus group. Upon conclusion of their review, participants returned the document to this researcher indicating if there were any inaccuracies related to transcription interpretation and member errors contained therein. This form of member validation provided credibility and ensured that the data captured was indeed what the participant conveyed.

Transferability

In an effort to establish the trustworthiness of this research study, transferability of research methods was demonstrated. Connelly (2016) defines transferability as the manner in which research is useful and applicable to others within their personal context. In order to achieve transferability this researcher provided vivid descriptions (Carcary, 2009) of the research process, sufficient enough for readers and those within the research community to substantiate the findings' applicability and ultimately be able to replicate (Lishner, 2015) this study as deemed appropriate. Readers will find that this researcher has detailed each progressive step undertaken in answering this study's research questions. In addition, interview protocols (Appendix J) were utilized that provided a blueprint for the manner in which interviews were facilitated. This protocol included a step-by step chronological method for facilitating interviews from informing participants about the anticipated length of interviews to ensuring seating arrangements have been made. As such vivid descriptions detailing each step of this study and interview protocols aided in ensuring transferability of this research.

Dependability

It was the responsibility of this researcher to ensure that the methodological approach to capturing the data for the research was consistent, dependable and accurately reflected the reported data (Noble & Smith, 2015) within this study. Researchers have long sought to increase principles of dependability of which Lishner (2015) lists a myriad of recommendations (p.53) such as:

1. The collection of additional data based on promising initial results
2. The inclusion of a comprehensive literature review
3. The description of sample size selection procedures

In this qualitative descriptive study participants participated in interviews and additional data was collected through the facilitation of a focus group. A comprehensive literature review was included in this study that provides an exhaustive and in-depth examination of data surrounding this research topic. This included background data, information pertaining to the study's theoretical framework and the inter-connectivity of domestic violence advocacy, compassion fatigue and self-care strategies. An additional strategy to further solidify dependability of this research study, was to provide a detailed description of sample size procedures. This will be facilitated through meticulous documentation related to how site authorization was achieved, methods for sample recruitment and criteria dictating how this study's sample size was ultimately met. Each of these processes served as a layer of dependability achievement, for this research study.

Confirmability

According to Connelly (2016), confirmability is "the neutrality or the degree findings are consistent and could be repeated" (p.435). This researcher sought to confirm the authenticity of this research by ensuring outcomes were reproducible and manifested as consistent, to enable another researcher to follow the decision trail utilized by this researcher (Smith & McGannon, 2018; Elo, Kääriäinen, Kanste, Pölkki, Utriainen, & Kyngäs, 2014). As reported by Maher, Hadfield, Hutchings and de Eyto (2018), research is to be compiled in such a detailed manner that the research decision-making process, data collection and analysis is gathered with such dependability that research efforts may be duplicated and ultimately validated. In this research, confirmability was achieved by ensuring researcher neutrality and an iterative data analysis process. To demonstrate researcher objectivity, the limitations and assumptions of this study were chronicled in Chapter 3. A stringent data trail was compiled through the research process by detailing each step taken, as a means to create transparency and rigor as a demonstration of objectivity (Symon, Cassell & Johnson, 2018). Coding provided the opportunity to extract and analyze what participants shared related to self-care strategies in the prevention of compassion fatigue, ensuring that what was reported is authentically that of participants, devoid of researcher bias.

Data Collection and Management

The data collected for this study involved domestic violence advocates from the Mid-Atlantic region of the United States it was anticipated that twelve to fifteen (12-15) people would participate in interviews and six to eight (6-8) participants would engage in a focus group. The collection and management of data were considered one of the most integral components of the research process and without a stringent and methodical approach, the study conducted would not be authentically viable. This scholar had the benefit of participating in and completing the Collaborative Institutional Training Initiative (CITI) program, which provided comprehensive training on the intricacies, ethical considerations and knowledge base related to conducting research with human subject participants. Based on this information and awareness of research protocol and standards, permission was granted from Grand Canyon University Institutional Review Board (Appendix B) to facilitate this research. Prior to engaging in research protocols with the Institutional Review Board, Site Authorization had to granted. This researcher made contact with leadership from the organization where this study would be conducted and received Site Authorization (Appendix A) to recruit participants.

This initial contact with the Executive Director was made via email in order to establish a paper trail and documentation of communication with the organization. Once approval was granted from the organization, (Appendix A) a thorough explanation of the research process was presented to staff members, to include informed consent/confidentiality and ethical considerations related to participating in this proposed study. While the sample population for this research study was domestic violence advocates who were employed within the organization, eligibility of participants would need to be determined in order to ascertain which participants would engage in interviews and those who would participate in the focus group. This was achieved by sending an email to staff who were domestic violence advocates requesting that they participate in this study. A recruitment email (Appendix K) along with informed consent will be sent to the Executive Director with a request that that the email be distributed to staff who are domestic violence advocates. In order to diminish researcher selection bias, it was determined that the first 12-15 domestic violence advocates who respond to this researcher would participate in interviews and those that responded thereafter would be designated as focus group participants.

Subsequently, this researcher would be seeking twelve to fifteen (12-15) participants for the interview portion of this study, and six to eight (6-8) participants for the focus group. Participants would meet inclusion criteria in order to participate in this qualitative descriptive study 1) Serve as a domestic violence advocate employee within a domestic violence organization in the Mid-Atlantic region of the United States. 2) Have served in this capacity for approximately one year 3) Be over the age of 18 years old 4) Informed Consent/Confidentiality forms would be reviewed with each participant and their signed consent to include their printed name on the document, would serve as their willingness to participate in the focus group or complete a questionnaire for this research study. Each participant will sign the consent and return it to this scholar and appropriately secured. In order to implement confidentiality practices, each participant will be given a unique identifier in order to protect their privacy, with numerical codes assigned to each participant.

Interviews and a focus group, have been selected as data collection methodologies based on their examination nature, for it is through the questions asked in each of these forums that answers to this study's research questions may be explicated. As a central figure in elucidating this phenomenon, the questions asked in the interviews and focus group were constructed and tailored in such a deliberate manner that it would extract meaning and noteworthiness. Manzano (2016), cautions researchers on how they ask questions and places significant emphasis on phrasing and the manner in which questions are asked and written as the pursuit of meaning and knowledge is behind each question. Due to such weight being placed on these questions, and in order to fulfill this intention and achieve the objective of this study an expert panel was convened to comprehensively vet the questions for this research. Considered stakeholders within this particular field of research, these expert panelists are besought for their ability to synthesize and provide sound recommendations pertaining to the subject matter (Waltz et al, 2015) this approach is also considered an exemplary research strategy (Manzano, 2016).

In the construct and compilation of interview and focus group questions, expert panelists will explore, and certify the questions that will be posed to participants in order to give credence to these instruments. The methodology of implementing an expert panel at this particular junction in data collection, will add an additional layer of data saturation and seek to minimize and remove this researcher's, personal lens and bias (Fusch & Ness, 2015) during the interview and focus group process. For this research, the proposed interview and focus group questions were sent to seven (7) doctoral expert professionals of which three (3) (Appendix I) consented to participate as expert panelists for this proposed research study. All three (3) had terminal doctoral degrees and significant knowledge as either qualitative researchers or subject matter professionals. Expert panelists provided noteworthy feedback and ultimately indicated research questions were apropos for the study being conducted. However, in their review of research data questions, they did provide feedback, and the consensus rested upon the need to streamline questions in a chronological manner based on the theme, in order to achieve cohesion and flow.

Original questions (Appendix H) as compiled and developed by this researcher vacillated between themes which panelists conferred would not yield the responses desired to answer the research questions. In addition, expert panelists strongly recommended that the constructs of terminology such as compassion fatigue and self-care be operationalized. By proffering the question in this manner, it would prevent less ambiguity and generate the focus and specificity participants need in order to answer questions comprehensively and provide the depths in response this researcher is seeking. Expert panelists' feedback was incorporated in the compilation of a revised (Appendix J) version of research questions, that appear significantly more cohesive and will provide the depths needed to answer this proposed study's overall research question.

Not only were research questions for the data instruments reviewed by expert panelist advisers, but these questions were also vetted and solidified by field testers. This practice of testing out questions that will be asked of the sample population helps to ensure the responses will ultimately meet the targeted objective of the designated research questions. Interview and focus group questions were comprehensively vetted by those within the field, providing the opportunity for those within the profession but not part of the sample population to test the efficacy of each question being asked of participants. This researcher conducted field test interviews that ranged from 20-30 minutes, with several people in the field of domestic violence advocacy to practice focus group and interview questions. Many were eager to contribute to this capacity and provided salient feedback on the questions that were asked. It was indicated that some questions appeared redundant, and respondents felt as though they answered certain questions previously.

Research questions did provide the appearance of being redundant due to similar questions being asked related to compassion fatigue and then pertaining to self-care strategies. Participants did seek clarification on the definition of terminology utilized such as compassion fatigue and the meaning of self-care. Once they were able to ascertain the researcher and participants were on the same page pertaining to these terms, they were able to answer research questions with ease. The flow of the practice field testing yielded positive results and experience for participants who were eager to share their experiences related to this subject matter and its influence upon their profession. The process of field-testing research questions was beneficial in providing a medium in which this researcher could practice and have a pre-experiential opportunity prior to conducting legitimate questioning for this research.

Interviews

Participants that engage in the interview portion of this research will participate in a semi-structured interview process in order to answer research questions related to self-care strategies and how this protocol diminishes the impact of compassion fatigue. This researcher would ensure that informed consent is obtained at the onset of the interview. To facilitate interviews in a manner convenient for participants, several interview options will be presented in which they may select the method most appropriate for their schedule. Interview options such as face to face, videoconference or telephonic participation will be made available based on participant preference. Face to face interviews may be conducted at the organization or in a location convenient to the participant.

In this research study opportunities will be presented for participants to engage in interviews through video-conference mechanisms. There a plethora of platforms such as Zoom, GoToMeetings and Skype that can be utilized as convenient method for to capture data provided by participants. Weller (2017), LeBaron, Jarzabkowski, Pratt and Fetzer (2018), highlight digital communication and the role that it plays in social science research data collection, in the analysis of human behavior. In addition to video conferencing, participants will also be able to have interviews conducted via tele-conference. James (2016) mentions a caveat about this approach, as the researcher will need to be aware of the various data interpretation issues that may arise due to the lack of visual context, and nuances from participants that the researcher may not be able to observe with this telephonic approach. To ensure systematic uniformity throughout each interview it is beneficial to develop and utilize an interview guide (Goodell, Stage & Cooke, 2016) to serve as a script and protocol to adhere to in the facilitation of the interviews. Interviews will be semi-structured to include open-ended questions, which will allow room for the interviewer to further probe responses and interviewees to provide clarification of their answers. While questions presented in the interview will be pre-determined by this researcher, this forum will permit opportunities for participants to expound upon their responses (Percy, Kostere & Kostere, 2015).

Interview questions will commence with the collection of participant demographic information and segue into reflective questions based on the influence of self-care strategies in the prevention of compassion fatigue. At least 60 minutes will be allotted for each interview to take place which should be sufficient time for participants to share their lived experiences and insights related to self-care strategies and compassion fatigue. At this stage in the process, it will be incumbent upon this researcher to be cognizant of ensuring that data saturation is achieved from the responses provided by participants. According to Fusch and Ness (2015), an inability to achieve data saturation can deleteriously influence the validity of the research being conducted, as such it is imperative that this strategy is surveilled. Social science researchers have achieved consensus in the definition of data saturation as being achieved when there is no more new information to be gleaned from the population sample (Saldana, 2016; Saunders, Sim, Kingstone, Baker, Waterfield, Bartlam, ... & Jinks; 2018).

This researcher sought to conduct 12-15 interviews with domestic violence advocates and in the event that this sample size could not be achieved, this researcher would continue recruitment efforts in order to solidify this sample size. This would be facilitated by re-connecting with organizational leadership where the research planned to be conducted to make inquiries of the pool of participants to enlist in study efforts until the sample size would be fully achieved. Based on the 12-15 interview participants, a designation would be made as to when data saturation would be achieved based on interviews completed. This researcher designated that data saturation may occur after five (5) consecutive interviews are conducted and there is depth (Fusch &Ness, 2015) of data presented without any new information revealed. It is important to note, that even after data saturation is achieved that efforts would continue to complete remaining interviews in order to further augment the data obtained and have increased information to add to the breadth and scope of richness gleaned from all participants.

Upon the conclusion of the interviews, data management would commence. The audio recording of the interviews would be transcribed into a Micro-Soft Word document and participants would be able to facilitate a member check to verify the accuracy of statements provided. In addition to reviewing transcripts, participants would also receive a summary of the interview compiled by this researcher. This summary would present themes and patterns that have been obtained based on the responses participants have provided to this study's research questions. As such, participants would be given the manuscript of their interview in tandem with a summarization of important data that has been explicated for their review.

Considered a crucial component of qualitative research validity and a best practice (Candela, 2019), member checking enables participants, the opportunity to analyze and verify, that recorded responses indeed match the interpretation as recorded in data analysis (Varpio, Ajjawi, Monrouxe, O'brien & Rees, 2017).As a check and balance, according to Candela (2019), member checks provide the opportunity for participants to be reflective and establish cohesiveness with their personal experience. As such, in order to conduct member checking for this proposed research, contact would be made with each participant to establish a time to meet and a time designated, to have them review the transcript of their data and this researcher's summary of the interview that was facilitated. Upon their comprehensive assessment of the document containing their data, they would have the opportunity to provide feedback pertaining to elements they designate as a misrepresentation or misinterpretation of information shared within the confines of their interview.

Data collected would be secured in two separate locations to ensure these documents are properly safeguarded. The first location would be a lock box with a key within this researcher's home, and the second location would be in a lock box secured in a vault, at this researcher's financial institution. Data collected would be secured for a period of 4-5 years on two password-protected thumb drives kept in separate locations in order to ensure non-disclosure of data gleaned from participants. The interview portion of this study would seek to answer this study's research questions, in order to ascertain the influence typically utilized self-care strategies have on domestic violence advocates in the Mid-Atlantic region of the United States, who work with clients who are physically, mentally, sexually or financially abused, in preventing compassion fatigue.

Focus Group

Focus group participants would analyze themes from data collected from interviews. They would confirm or discount these themes in addition to adding any themes that may not have been obtained through the interview process. Focus group participants would have received the recruitment email from their organizations Executive Director. The email would include the informed consent, with a request for it to be reviewed, signed and returned to this researcher prior to scheduling the focus group. Once all informed consents are received, this researcher would contact all participants for the focus group to gain consensus on the date and time most conducive to schedule the focus group. During this initial contact, the request to audio record the focus group would be made. Once permission is granted from all participants, scheduling would be complete. Based on the needs of participants the focus group would take place in a conference room within the organization or if more desirable, in a location outside of the organization in a public facility such as a community library.

The focus group would require face to face participation with this researcher serving as a moderator for the focus group, enabling participants the liberty to disclose, dialogue and contemplate the research questions as assigned. With over ten (10) years' experience as a Certified Family Partnership Meeting Facilitator, this researcher was well equipped in group engagement and facilitation procedures, to include managing group behavior and dynamics, such as those that may present in a focus group. According to Newcomer, Hatry and Wholey (2015), focus group moderators are skilled in providing an environment where participants feel comfortable sharing, aid in welcoming diverse views and help participants build upon what is disclosed, as they describe their thoughts on the focus group subject matters. In a similar manner, Family Partnership Meeting Facilitators engage with participants and navigate complex group dynamics (Kim, Pierce, Jaggers, Imburgia & Hall, 2016) and subsequently **Family Partnership Meeting Facilitators** skill-level in facilitation has contributed to the success of group meetings.

Prior to the commencement of the focus group, introductory remarks will be made to participants related to focus group procedures and expectations. A semi-structured format would provide sufficient opportunity for participants to delve into the research topic of self-care in the prevention of compassion fatigue within the scope and perspective of their domestic violence advocacy responsibilities. Just as in interviews, open-ended questions would be presented during the focus group with an unstructured approach permitting opportunities for this researcher to follow up and gain clarification where deemed appropriate. Questions posed to participants would be focused on understanding typically utilized self-care techniques and the influence of self-care strategies on domestic violence advocates in preventing compassion fatigue.

This researcher would utilize the checklist guide prepared in advance of the focus group, in order to ensure that all criteria and expectations outlined for the focus group have adhered too. Open-ended questions that are progressive in nature would be posed to participants in order to commence the focus group in a jocund manner with the deliberate intent for the discussion to evolve into the profundities related to self-care and compassion fatigue within this profession. This would coincide with the themes generated in interviews and participants will validate and expound upon data previously collected. While questions presented in the focus group would be pre-determined by this researcher this forum will permit opportunities for participants to expound upon their responses or that of fellow participants (Percy, Kostere & Kostere, 2015).

The estimated timeframe allotted for the focus group would be between 1-2 hours, providing sufficient time for participants to comprehensively dialogue regarding the questions posed. In a similar vein that the interviews were conducted, and data saturation achieved, likewise within the context of the focus group data saturation must be ascertained during the process. Fusch and Ness (2015), pronounce that data saturation is accomplished when no new information can be obtained, and it is no longer feasible for additional coding to take place. Whereas with interviews, it is proposed that data saturation will take place after five (5) interviews with no new data presented, however, within the realm of the focus group the approach is slightly altered. This researcher can project that data saturation may occur during the focus group when **according to Hennink,**

Kaiser and Weber (2019) redundancy begin to occur and no further data manifests from focus group participants.

This researcher compiled a thematic code grid (Appendix L) based on themes from interviews and during the focus group notations would be made for each of these themes and any additional themes that manifest. Data saturation will be satisfied when according to Saldana (2016) there is no new information and further coding is no longer feasible (Fusch & Ness, 2015). In the event that the designated sample size cannot be achieved, this researcher will continue recruitments efforts in order to solidify this sample size for the focus group. This will be facilitated by re-connecting with organizational leadership where the research is being conducted and inquiring of the pool of participants to enlist in study efforts until the sample size is fully achieved. In addition, this researcher may recruit participants from additional family violence centers that employ domestic violence advocates, in the event a sufficient sample size cannot be obtained from the original family violence center this researcher recruited participants from.

Upon conclusion of the focus group, data management will commence in tandem with the interviews. The audio recording of the focus group will be transcribed into a Micro-Soft Word document and a summary of themes and patterns will be provided, where participants will be able to facilitate a member check to verify the accuracy of statements provided. Similar to the member checks facilitated for interviews, respondent validation will also take place amongst focus group participants. Saunders (2018), indicates that member checking within the qualitative realm lends to the trustworthiness of the research conducted and that participants are ensured that their words and experiences are reflected (Birt et al. 2016), and not that of the researcher.

For this proposed research, once the data is transcribed and a summary compiled, this researcher will reach out to each focus group participant to make arrangements for them to review the data and provide feedback, affirmation and validation that their responses were captured accordingly. This respondent validation will ensure that recorded responses match the interpretation as recorded in data analysis (Varpio, Ajjawi, Monrouxe, O'brien & Rees, 2017). Data collected will be secured in two separate locations for a period of 4-5 years on two password-protected thumb drives kept in separate locations in order to ensure non-disclosure of data gleaned from participants.

Data Analysis Procedures

This qualitative descriptive study seeks to elucidate the influence of self-care in the prevention of compassion fatigue in domestic violence advocates in the Mid-Atlantic region of the United States. Specifically, this study's research questions sought to answer, which self-care techniques are typically used by domestic violence advocates in the Mid-Atlantic region of the United States, and the influence these self-care strategies have on domestic violence advocates in preventing compassion fatigue. The following research questions were carefully crafted and developed to ensure the phenomenon could be captured and answered by these questions:

RQ1: What self-care techniques do domestic violence advocates from the Mid-Atlantic region of the United States, describe as typically used in the prevention of compassion fatigue?

RQ2: How do domestic violence advocates from the Mid-Atlantic region of the United States use self-care to prevent compassion fatigue?

Interviews and a focus group will be utilized as data collection sources in order to answer the phenomenon being studied. Participants who complete interviews and the focus group would disclose information on self-care strategies typically utilized, and their influence in the prevention of compassion fatigue. Information generated would provide participant perspective on the degree in which they perceive self-care strategies aid in the prevention of compassion fatigue and how they seek self-regulation through the use of self-care. Rich data and themes related to elucidating the phenomenon of self-care in the prevention of compassion fatigue within this sample population will manifest from this data analysis.

A thorough analysis of the data collected from the interviews and focus group will be thematically analyzed. Considered, by researchers to be one of the most complex components of qualitative research, data analysis needs to be facilitated in a thoroughly transparent manner to ensure readers are able to conceptualize the process undertaken by the researcher (Nowell, Norris, White & Moules, 2017). According to Elo et al. (2014), the presentation of data analysis in a sequential and logical manner is critical to the research study as it supports the evaluation of the results and therefore establishes reliability and trustworthiness. This will generate patterns of rich data collected from the methodological approaches of the interviews and focus group in order to answer the research questions, this study proposes. Within the body of qualitative research design, the primary focus is to conceptualize and glean meaningfulness from words through the recognition of patterns while maintaining the integrity of the dimensionality within its context (Leung, 2015).

Interviews and Focus Group

For this study data from interviews and the focus group will be transcribed by Rev Enterprises (Rev.com) by transcribing data from audio to Microsoft Word in order for thematic analysis (Gough & Lyons, 2016) and coding to commence. After transcription is complete this researcher will proofread documents as many times as needed to ensure accuracy. Upon completion of this task, this researcher will provide each participant with a copy via email of the Microsoft Word transcribed document in order for member checking to occur, which according to Varpio, Ajjawi, Monrouxe, O'brien and Rees, (2017) provides a checks and balance wherein participants are given the opportunity to analyze and verify that recorded responses indeed match the interpretation as recorded in data analysis. This practice can aid in diminishing elements of misrepresentation and misinterpretation of their stated facts and this process helps to support the establishment of credibility.

Once member checks have been returned and all revisions duly noted, and final approval granted by participants of the transcription, this researcher will review the transcript once again for verifiability and then move forward with thematic analysis. This researcher will utilize the support of technology to aid in the meticulous task of analyzing data for themes and patterns related to the research questions. NVivo considered one of the premier tools utilized in qualitative data software analysis (O'Neill, Sarah, & Lamb,2018), will specialize in thematic analysis and the organization of this data. This researcher will ascribe to the six phases of thematic analysis as outlined by Nowell, Norris, White & Moules (2017) to answer the phenomenon for this study;

1. The familiarization of the data
2. Generation of initial codes

3. Search for themes
4. Review of themes
5. Defining and naming themes
6. Production of the report

The familiarization of the data - prior to and after member checks, this researcher will begin the process of familiarization of the data by reading the transcriptions multiple times, this will allow for absorption of the material and a conscientious understanding of the data collected. Based on this knowledge base and familiarity, a broad level of coding (Weis & Willems, 2017) can commence which enables the initial steps of moving the data from abstract to concrete. 2) *Generation of initial codes* - data is then assigned to a relevant code "when it captures the qualitative richness of the phenomenon" (Nowell et al. 2017, p.6) and data not considered relevant to answering the research question will not be discarded but relegated to the side (Nowell et al. 2017) and referred back to as needed. This practice of coding relevant data is the primary step in the development of establishing patterns in respondent answers, which will then segue into themes generated from within the transcriptions to determine whether these items are relevant to the research questions. According to Nowell, Norris, White and Moules (2017), "A theme is an abstract entity that brings meaning and identity to a recurrent experience and its variant manifestations. As such, a theme captures and unifies the nature or basis of the experience into a meaningful whole" (pg.8).

3)*Search for themes* - through a thorough analysis of the codes, different themes will emerge that will result in separate clusters of information based on similarities amongst the data. The process of coding and thematic analysis will be iterative in nature (Nowell, Norris, White & Moules, 2017), with the study in a continued state of review manifesting to evaluate themes for appropriateness and relevance as it pertains to the research question. A determination will be made to siphon away those codes that do not apply or subsume those that fit into the themes that arise from the data collected. Codes that are inter-related will be grouped together, and re-classified under a sub-theme that encapsulates and summarizes the totality of the group categories. Once themes are designated then the task is assigned to provide each theme with a name that is apropos and fully encapsulates the codes assigned to the grouping of themes.

4) *Review of themes*-during this phase the researcher engages in continuous review of the data evaluating thematic concepts that may manifest. Themes may begin to emerge at this time in an unrefined manner derived from the data ranging from specific to broad, providing a rough draft of the research story. It is at this time; this researcher may notice new codes emerging that will need to categorize thematically based on relevancy. A clear pattern becomes evident as to how the data segues into a code, and then develops into a theme.

5) *Defining and naming themes* is considered a period of further refinement and is a phase that can be challenging to assess when sufficient thematic analysis has occurred. A consultation with committee members will take place in an iterative manner to determine if this researcher has exhausted thematic analysis and that all themes are clearly defined and named. 6) *Production of the report* is considered the sixth phase of thematic analysis is comprised of writing the narrative that tells the story garnered from data collection and analysis. This account will include direct quotes from respondents that further chronicles the route to achieved outcomes (Nowell, Norris, White & Moules, 2017), related to self-care in the prevention of compassion fatigue. As reported by

Twining, Heller, Nussbaum and Tsai, (2017), each element in data analysis should be influenced by the need to create saturation, which is developed once thorough an exhaustive examination of the codes, themes, and patterns of the data collected (Appendix J). In an effort to ensure accuracy related to coding processes and thematic material, this researcher will juxtapose coding material from this proposed research alongside Saldana (2016), a highly sought after and notable resource within the social science and qualitative realm.

Limitations and Delimitations

According to Marshall and Rossman (2016), there is no perfect research design, subsequently, throughout the course of this research, there may be several assumptions, limitations and delimitations that influence aspects of this research.

Limitations

Pyrczak (2016) reports that limitations are weaknesses that may be found within the research that goes beyond the control and authority of the researcher and these limitations could potentially impact and call into question the validity of the study outcome. In addition, within the facilitation of research, there are assumptions made, which are principles frequently taken for granted by the researcher, about the proposed research (Lindlof & Taylor, 2017). Within this study, only generalizations can be made to this population as all other populations were excluded from participating in this study. In addition, only one theoretical framework will be utilized for this study, whereas additional constructs may have added supplementary insight and information on the subject matter.

Participants for this study will be limited to those who work at the domestic violence organization where the study is to be conducted in the Mid-Atlantic region of the United States subsequently, excluding those from other domestic violence-related organizations throughout the entire United States. Rich data from other entities will not be gleaned and therefore no additional noteworthy contributions made. In addition, the organization where the research will be facilitated does not have a large amount of staff and therefore the sample size will be small, due to limited staffing beyond this researchers' control. Another noteworthy limitation relates to time constraints in which to conduct this research. This study will be conducted over a limited amount of time and subsequently will only be able to capture data over a short span of time and data obtained will only be gleaned from a short time frame. It should also be noted that this field is a female-dominated industry and subsequently most of the participants for this proposed research will be female, preventing a comprehensive gender perspective. It would be beneficial to know the male perspective as it relates to self-care and evaluate the difference between gender and self-care care interventions utilized.

Delimitations

Delimitations are within the purview of the researcher and refer to the boundaries of the study as imposed and specifically chosen by the researcher that is intentionally omitted in order to ensure the manageability and construct of the proposed research (Ellis & Levy, 2009). The following researcher-imposed constrictions were excluded in the fulfillment of this study;

1. The selection size of the sample is limited to one organization wherein, this researcher has purposely chosen to utilize only one domestic violence organization instead of including several family violence institutions from the Mid-Atlantic region of the United States, within the body of this research.

2. The use of a qualitative research methodology instead of quantitative, which could possibly capture measurements of data that qualitative findings may not be able to provide.
3. The selection of domestic violence advocates as research participants and the subsequent exclusion of domestic violence survivors and the void their perspective may bring to this proposed research.
4. As it relates to the sources of data utilized for this study, the use of observations and field notes were deselected as data collection measures, due to the intrusive and intense nature of these approaches.

To address and minimize the challenges presented by this study's limitations and delimitations, this researcher will employ proactive and preventative strategies to ensure the solubility of this research. Despite the small sample size, participants for this study purposely will consist of an eclectic range of employees, in order to obtain a diverse set of opinions and perspectives in which to influence data outcomes. Interview and focus group questions will be diligently constructed by this researcher and vetted by a cross-section of expert panelists who will contribute to the study by thoroughly examining research questions to ensure appropriateness and removal of bias, for this study. Coulter, Elfenbaum, Jain and Jonas (2016), indicate that incorporating an expert panelist is another methodical approach that can add insight when conducting research, along with field testing. In addition, member checks are considered one of the most crucial techniques for establishing credibility (Varpio, Ajjawi, Monrouxe, O'brien & Rees, 2017) as it provides a degree of checks and balances required for evidence-based research.

Assumptions

Within the facilitation of research, there are assumptions made, which are principles frequently taken for granted by the researcher, about the proposed research (Lindlof & Taylor, 2017). There are assumptions made as it pertains to this research related to honesty, confidentiality and the knowledge base of participants. It is assumed that participants will be transparent in answering research questions in disclosing the influence of self-care in the prevention of compassion fatigue. It is assumed that participants in the focus group will keep what is discussed within the confines of the group confidential and will not share with others what participants have disclosed in the group. It can also be assumed that participants will have a cursory knowledge of self-care and be aware of compassion fatigue which are focal points of this proposed research study.

Summary

This chapter focused on the approach that will be utilized to facilitate this qualitative descriptive study in the quest to examine the influence of self-care in the prevention of compassion fatigue on domestic violence advocates. The research methodology is an integral component of this research study, for it would be implausible to answer the research question without a comprehensive outline of how this may be achieved. In review, this chapter provided a synopsis of the problem statement, related to the phenomenon of self-care and this research sample population, as empirical data supports the need for further research on the subject of self-care strategies and domestic violence advocates (Alani & Stroink, 2015).

Out of this problem statement, manifested two research questions that belied the need for further in-depth study in order to answer these queries and advance scientific knowledge. In order to do so, a qualitative (Bowen, 2010) methodological approach was chosen due to the emphasis on meaning, interpretation (Gough & Lyons, 2016; Levitt, Bamberg, Creswell, Frost, Josselson & Suárez-Orozco, 2018)) and the multimodal data sources with Gough and Lyons, (2016) reporting that qualitative research supports the development of psychological knowledge. Based on this approach a descriptive study research design was selected as it would best and most comprehensively answer the designated research questions. According to Kim, Sefcik and Bradway (2017), qualitative descriptive studies are considered important and are frequently utilized when research questions seek to answer, "the who, what, and where of events or experiences and gaining insights from informant (p. 1)".

It was determined that interviews and a focus group would be the most suitable instruments for this proposed study. The semi-structured approach of interviews provides the ability for the researcher to probe further into responses and provides the room for participants to elaborate as needed (Percy, Kostere & Kostere, 2015). Researchers Guest, Namey, Taylor, Eley and McKenna (2017) have indicated that the interactive structure and information nature of focus groups, often provide richer data than what single participants can produce. The designated target population for this study are domestic violence advocates from a family violence organization in the Mid-Atlantic region of the United States, with domestic violence advocates participating in interviews and focus groups. Through informed consent, participants will be given assurance of their privacy and confidentiality (Wolf, Patel, Tarver, Austin, Dame & Beskow, 2015) for participating in this research. This chapter also elaborated on the need to achieve trustworthiness within the research methodology in order to ensure rigor, to include transferability, credibility, consistency and dependability (Lub, 2015; Cypress, 2017; Noble & Smith, 2015).

This chapter explored the importance of meticulous detail in data collection, management and thematic analysis as core components utilized to achieve and maintain research validity and reliability. Marshall and Rossman (2016), proffer that there is no perfect research design, subsequently, limitations, delimitations and assumptions are presented in this chapter, along with highlights of ethical considerations (Noyes et al., 2018) that may arise through the facilitation of this research proposal. The next chapter will elaborate on the actualization of the measures discussed in this chapter, to include a comprehensive presentation of the methodological approach of data collection and the conclusive findings of the analyzed data. In addition, chapter 4 will provide the results of this proposed study in response to the research question, the various themes that may emerge through the evaluative process. Tables and figures will also be presented to visually demonstrate and support research material and findings within this qualitative research.

Chapter 4: Data Analysis and Results

Introduction

Domestic violence is a major public health epidemic and within the United States it is reported that 5 million women are abused annually (Macy, Martin, Nwabuzor Ogbonnaya & Rizo, 2018). Domestic violence advocates serve on the front line engaging those who are traumatized by violence and due to the chronic exposure (Sansbury, Graves & Scott, 2015) they experience compassion fatigue. Self-care is considered an invaluable resource (Bressi & Vaden, 2017) that can be utilized to address compassion fatigue. However, there is limited research on the intersectionality of self-care, compassion fatigue and domestic violence advocates. As such, the purpose of this study was to explore how domestic violence advocates who work with physically, mentally, sexually or financially abused clients in the Mid-Atlantic region of the United States, described the influence of self-care in the prevention of compassion fatigue.

The research design used for this study was of a qualitative descriptive nature, and as reported by Kim, Sefcik and Bradway (2017), studies using this approach are considered important and are frequently utilized when research questions seek to answer, "the who, what, and where of events or experiences and gaining insights from informant" (p. 1). This research focused on domestic violence advocates employed in family violence organizations in various states throughout the Mid-Atlantic region of the United States. This study manifested to answer the following two (2) research questions.

> **RQ1**: What self-care techniques do domestic violence advocates from the Mid-Atlantic region of the United States describe as typically being used in the prevention of compassion fatigue?

RQ2: How do domestic violence advocates from the Mid-Atlantic region of the United States use self-care to prevent compassion fatigue?

This chapter will provide detailed information on how data analysis occurred and the outcome of research results. Information presented in this chapter will consist of steps utilized in preparation for data analysis, narrative summary of participants, descriptive data and a summary of the results obtained in addition to notable changes from what was proposed in Chapter 3.

Important Changes and Updates to Information in Chapters 1-3

In the data collection phase of this study, changes were made that were not originally anticipated as proposed in Chapter 3. These changes are highlighted and reflected in the following section. Initially, this learner anticipated that all study participants would be readily obtained from one domestic violence organization within the Mid-Atlantic region of the United States. A preliminary consent had been granted from the organization's leadership and subsequently permission was sought through IRB, with approval subsequently fully granted.

As outlined in Chapter 3, this researcher requested that the domestic violence organization's Executive Director send an email to all domestic violence advocates with the request that they accept participation in this study by contacting this researcher. However, at the onset of data collection only two (2) advocates responded to the request to participate in this study. This researcher determined that to achieve data saturation, additional domestic violence organizations would need to be queried regarding their willingness to allow their advocates to participate.

In an exhaustive online search of domestic violence organizations within the Mid-Atlantic region of the United States, emails were sent to over thirty (30) agencies that employed domestic violence advocates. Included in each email was an overview of the study, Site Authorization Letter, and the Informed Consent for prospective participants to review. There were many barriers that preempted organizations from participating in this study pertaining to the influence of self-care in the prevention of compassion fatigue. Due to the Covid-19 pandemic, domestic violence organizations and requests for the services they provide were at an all-time high due to the national escalation of domestic violence incidents (hotline.org, N.D.).

Subsequently, many agencies, were short-staffed, advocates were working from home, and data collection was scheduled to take place during the holiday season, when advocates were occupied during this peak season of meeting victim and children needs. As such, many agencies declined to participate in this research study, or stated that they would be willing to revisit participation at another time. This researcher continued efforts to locate participants, and successfully recruited three (3) additional organizations wherein advocates could engage in the data collection process. A total of four (4) organizations provided Site Authorization (Appendix A), and this researcher sought and obtained Institutional Review Board (IRB) approval (Appendix B) to conduct research with advocates from these domestic violence organizations. Pseudonyms were assigned to the names of the four (4) domestic violence organizations that provided site authorizations for their advocates to be recruited to participate in this research study and are listed as follows.

- Evolutions Domestic Peace Organization (Virginia)

- Innovative Path Center (Virginia)
- Progeny Incorporated Inc (Delaware)
- Evangelical Resolution Home (Pennsylvania)

While this researcher initially forecasted that all interview and focus group participants would come from one organization, challenges that arose from recruiting, resulted in a total of thirteen (13) semi-structured interviews being conducted, with nine (9) from one organization Evolutions Domestic Peace Organization, Virginia, three (3) from Progeny Incorporated, Delaware, and one (1) from Evangelical Resolution Home, Philadelphia, another domestic violence organization, all within the Mid-Atlantic region of the United States. All six (6) advocates who participated in the focus group originated from one agency Innovative Path Center, in Virginia and were all co-workers from the same organization.

This study utilized a purposive sampling approach to recruit participants to answer research questions. In addition, to this method, an unscripted change occurred that resulted in additional participants being recruited. As study participants who were recruited for this study through a purposive sampling approach, engaged in interviews, they shared with other advocates about this research and encouraged their co-workers to contact this researcher. Therefore, in addition to purposive sampling this research also utilized snowballing as a recruitment approach.

Another notable change related to the transcription source this researcher sought to utilize for this study. It was originally indicated in Chapter 3 that Rev.com would be utilized for transcription of interviews. However, once interviews were complete and transcription needed to occur, this researcher chose instead to utilize another source. Otter.ai was selected as a more precise and highly reviewed transcription service. In addition, the transcription fee for Otter.ai was more economical and a cost-effective resource for this researcher to utilize for this service.

A notable change from what was proposed in Chapter 3 related to data analysis, and the tool that would be utilized to accomplish this process. The use of technology to achieve data analysis were initially determined to be the best option, however, upon completion of data collection and transcription, a change was made. Instead of using Nvivo, this researcher determined that hand coding and analysis was the most optimal approach as it provided the opportunity to fully emerge in the data transcribed and collected. This process provided the best outcome for this research study as the time spent learning how to utilize Nvivo was instead spent being familiarized with the data and responses given by study participant

Preparation of Raw Data for Analysis and Descriptive Data

The phenomenon explored in this research sought to describe the influence of self-care in the prevention of compassion fatigue in domestic violence advocates. To answer the research questions as delineated in this study, advocates from domestic violence organizations from the Mid-Atlantic region of the United States were recruited for data collection purposes. Data collection was facilitated via semi-structured individual interviews and a focus group, with a total of nineteen (19) participants actively engaged in answering the research questions posed to them for this study.

Over the course of forty-eight (48) days from 2020-2021, data were collected. The sources utilized to capture data were semi-structured interviews and a focus group. It was predetermined that data would be collected either in-person, telephonically or via videoconferencing. Subsequently, all data collection took place via videoconferencing via

Zoom ® videoconferencing software. In order to recruit advocates that would be willing to participate in this study to determine the influence of self-care in the prevention of compassion fatigue in domestic violence advocates, initial outreach took place via email to the executive directors of various domestic violence organizations in the Mid-Atlantic region. The email explained the purpose of the study (Appendix D) and criteria needed for participation. Once the designated executive in charge of the domestic violence organization gave signed permission for a study to be conducted with their advocates, Institutional Review Board (IRB) approval was sought and granted. At that time, the recruitment form (Appendix K) was forwarded to advocates by their leadership with the request that interested advocates email this researcher to schedule a date and time of their convenience for the videoconference interview to be held.

The Informed Consent included information on the eligibility criteria to participate in the study to include, being over the age of 18 years old, employed as domestic violence advocate while serving as an advocate at a domestic violence organization in the Mid-Atlantic region of the United States. To ensure the interviews were facilitated in an organized and systematic manner, an Interview Protocol (Appendix I) was developed and adhered too. A total of thirteen (13) interviews were scheduled and recorded with the video captured on a secure laptop computer and saved on a secured USB drive. Upon completion of the interview each recording was electronically uploaded to Rev.com (Rev.com, n.d.) to be transcribed. Subsequently, the names of each participant were changed, and each advocate given a unique identifier, wherein each participant was labeled a number from one to nineteen (1-19). Interviews ranged from 18 minutes to 59 minutes, with an average length of 42 minutes for 13 semi-structured interviews, this information was captured in the semi-structured interview data set (Table 1)

Table 1

Semi-Structured Interview Dataset

Participant	Date	Duration	Page Length
1	12/29/2020	45:54	9
2	12/29/2020	57:50	12
3	12/30/2020	56:38	18
4	12/31/2020	59:12	20
5	1/4/2021	57:59	10
6	1/5/2021	26:57	7
7	12/30/2021	18:33	6
8	1/8/2021	44:46	11
9	1/13/2021	28:49	7
10	1/20/2021	28:49	6
11	1/25/2021	28:07	7
12	2/1/2021	42:48	10
13	2/18/2021	50:10	12

At the onset of the interview for Participant #7, the advocate reported not feeling well. The participant was asked if they would like to reschedule for a date and time when physical health improved. However, Participant # 7, declined to reschedule, preferring to proceed with the interview. Despite appearing rushed in answering the research questions posed, the responses provided by Participant # 7 were considered noteworthy and contributed saliently to this research study. In addition, interviews facilitated by Participants 9, 10 and 11 were less than 30 minutes. While it appeared, each advocate was actively engaged in the interview process, and they answered each interview question, their responses were not as lengthy as other participants. Despite this researcher asking following up questions with the expectation that these participants would disclose additional information, these interviews remained truncated in length. In contrast to the other participants, whose interviews were lengthier, the responses from the shortened interviews were still considered noteworthy.

All other interviews were facilitated as scheduled, and without any issues or noteworthy challenges. Each interview was transcribed for a total 135 pages, with each transcript averaging 10 pages in length. The focus group included six (6) Advocates and lasted for a total of 1 hour and 54 minutes, with a total of 28 transcribed pages as captured in the focus group dataset (Table 2). As each interview was transcribed, they were then sent to each participant via email in order for member checking to occur. Considered a crucial component of qualitative research validity and a best practice (Candela, 2019), member checking enables participants, the opportunity to analyze and verify, that recorded responses indeed match the interpretation as recorded in data analysis (Varpio, Ajjawi, Monrouxe, O'brien & Rees, 2017).

Table 2

Focus Group Dataset

Data Source	# Participants	Date	Length of Time	Transcript Length (Single-Spaced)
Focus Group	6	1/4/2021	01:54:41	28

Advocates were given a specific timeframe of 5-7 days to review and validate or clarify as deemed appropriate the transcript and then have it returned to this researcher. Advocates were notified via email that in the event transcripts were not returned within the allotted time, the transcripts would be considered approved by the interview participants. Several Advocates participated in elements of member checking by reviewing the transcripts of their semi-structured individual interviews. In returning the transcripts for member checking, this researcher did not summarize important meanings and request feedback from participants. Not doing so, may be considered a study limitation, expounded upon further in Chapter 5.

Upon return of transcripts, participants did not note any issues related to the misrepresentation or misinterpretation of information shared within the confines of their interview. The primary concerns relayed in member checking were shared by advocates who participated in the focus group. Participants expressed concern with discourse markers and wanting to remove those linguistic filler words from the focus group transcript. Focus group participants inquired whether they could have removed from the transcript those filler words that were ascribed to them throughout the transcript.

All advocates were over the age of eighteen and employed at local domestic violence organizations located in the Mid-Atlantic region of the United States. While all participants are considered advocates, who worked with victims of domestic violence, some of them held different titles and had assorted functions within the domestic violence organization they served. The majority of study participants were titled as Survivor Advocates, while other participant titles ranged from being a Hotline Team Lead, Lethality Assessment Protocol Coordinator, Emergency Shelter Coordinator, Community Advocate, Program Manager, Assistant Director and a Bilingual Survivor Advocate. This information is captured in Table 3 along with the regions where study participants came from.

Table 3

Study Participant Location & Advocate Title

Participant	Domestic Violence Organization	Participant State	Advocate Title
1.	Evolutions Domestic Peace Organization	Virginia	Community Advocate
2.	Evolutions Domestic Peace Organization	Virginia	Housing Advocate
3.	Progeny Incorporated	Delaware	Associate Director
4.	Evolutions Domestic Peace Organization	Virginia	Program Manager
5.	Evolutions Domestic Peace Organization	Virginia	Court/Survivor Advocate
6.	Evolutions Domestic Peace Organization	Virginia	Hotline Advocate/Team Lead
7.	Evolutions Domestic Peace Organization	Virginia	Latinx Survivor Advocate
8.	Evolutions Domestic Peace Organization	Virginia	Shelter Manager
9.	Evolutions Domestic Peace Organization	Virginia	Trauma Therapist
10.	Progeny Incorporated	Delaware	County Coordinator
11.	Evangelical Resolution Home	Virginia	Assistant Program Director
12.	Evolutions Domestic Peace Organization	Virginia	Survivor Advocate
13.	Progeny Incorporated	Virginia	Volunteer Coordinator
14.	Innovative Path Center	Virginia	Executive Director
15.	Innovative Path Center	Virginia	Advocacy Services Coordinator
16.	Innovative Path Center	Virginia	Outreach Volunteer and Outreach Coordinator
17.	Innovative Path Center	Virginia	Residential and Community Services Coordinator/Shelter Manager
18.	Innovative Path Center	Virginia	Director Client Services
19.	Innovative Path Center	Virginia	Court Advocate/Lethality Assessment Protocol Coordinator

While there were two over-arching research questions that guided this study's search to answer the gap in literature pertaining to the influence of self-care in the prevention of compassion fatigue, in total there were 12 questions asked to study participants. Research question number 1 had 8 questions and research question 2 had four questions. In the midst of collecting data, this researcher consistently evaluated for data saturation. This phenomenon occurred when there was no new information to be gleaned from interview and focus group participants (Saldana, 2016; Saunders et al.2018) and that indeed, an adequate sample size had been achieved (Hennink & Kaiser, 2021). Considered a vital milestone of data collection, the trustworthiness of this research study would have been deleteriously compromised (Fusch & Ness, 2015) without the achievement of data saturation. According to Hennink and Kaiser (2021), with regards to interviews, data saturation can be achieved within the range of 9-17 interviews, and for this study this researcher determined that there was no new data to be extrapolated at the conclusion of the tenth (10) interview. This researcher achieved data saturation when similar findings manifested and no new data emerged from the transcripts, according to the operational criteria as set forth by Islam and Aldaihani, (2022). As an additional level of surety, three (3) additional interviews were facilitated for a total of 13 semi-structured interviews. It is important to note that no new codes emerged from these interviews which helped to solidify the achievement of data saturation.

Upon review of the transcripts (Appendix O), coding commenced which resulted into grouped categories and emerging themes. As a cornerstone of rigor (Hennink & Kaiser, 2021), data saturation was successfully achieved for this research study, as all interviews were subsequently completed with no additional information gleaned from this sample population (Saldana, 2016; Saunders et al.2018). Consent was granted by each participant for their interview to be video recorded. Once this process was completed unique identifiers were given to each participant to ensure confidentiality and privacy of the information shared in interviews. Each interview was recorded and captured by Zoom © online videoconferencing software. At the conclusion of each interview, the recording for the interview was saved on a password protected laptop. Data analysis needed to take place and that would first need to be accomplished by transcribing each interview. This researcher utilized the transcription service of Otter.ai® a technology company that utilizes artificial intelligence to produce speech to text transcription of recordings (Otter.ai, 2022).

Each interview was transcribed in a Microsoft Word document, sent to this researcher, and then secured on an encrypted USB disk. The transcripts were reviewed several times for accuracy as this researcher listened to the videorecording while reading the transcripts. A comparison assessment was conducted to ensure precisely what participants shared on the video recording was captured correctly on each transcript. Through this process it was determined that all information shared by participants was fully accounted for and no data was missing.

In the quest to answer the research question regarding the influence of self-care in the prevention of compassion fatigue in domestic violence advocates, two overarching research questions set the foundation for this study delineated as RQ1, and RQ2. Subsequently, all participants were asked a total of twelve (12) questions in the interviews, and in the focus group (Appendix J). Each question was thoroughly vetted by an Expert Panel that was convened for the sole purpose of validating interview questions (Manzano, 2016). Eight (8) questions and their responses were attributed to RQ1, while four (4) questions were directed at answering RQ2. Questions 1-8 helped to answer RQ1 and questions 9-12, responded to RQ2.

Data Analysis Procedures

This qualitative descriptive study sought to answer the research question regarding the influence of self-care in the prevention of compassion fatigue in domestic violence advocates. Chapter 3 outlined the proposed data analysis procedures that would be facilitated for this research study. Whereas, an assortment of data analysis options could have been utilized, this researcher selected thematic analysis as the best approach to analyze data for this research study. According to Majumdar (2022), thematic analysis produces an intricate and detailed data set, that is rich, while yet being considered as a more flexible approach, in comparison to other data analysis methodologies.

Reflexivity Protocol

As part of reflexivity, the examination of this researcher's role is an integral component in establishing trustworthiness. Addressing reflexivity is essential, as it serves as a checks and balance ensuring that researcher bias and preconceptions, do not permeate or impede the analysis of data. There are numerous reflexivity protocols such as audit trails, bracketing and reflective journaling (Eryilmaz, 2021), that can be utilized to bolster research trustworthiness. This researcher did not utilize the aforementioned reflexivity models, but instead chose to conduct reflexivity and peer-review methods, by engaging in **qualitative research group discussion boards, peer review of research data to assess for researcher bias and contamination of data.** Reflexivity throughout the dissertation process, was an ongoing process that required this researcher to reflect inwardly on how this role influenced the research process (Treharne & Riggs, 2014).

Although this researcher attempted to be conscientious about predispositions influencing this study, it was important to acknowledge the role that axiological bias and values (Moroi, 2021) played within this study. This researcher's professional values as a domestic violence advocate could not be avoided and reflexivity would not offset the influence of axiology within this study; however, steps were incorporated to have this study evaluated in a reflective manner. The following peer review practices were deployed in attempts to assess for, and diminish researcher bias. Prior to data analysis this researcher joined qualitative discussion boards, such as, the Qualitative Study group, Grand Canyon University Doctoral Students, Grand Canyon University Doctoral Dissertation Milestones Support, wherein generalized data analysis processes were discussed, and feedback provided within groups. In addition, as a professional working in the domestic violence advocacy realm, this researcher was able to confer with colleagues about data analysis. This researcher sent two (2) colleagues this researcher's data analysis process, which consisted of Braun and Clarke (2006), six-step data analysis process and how this researcher conducted thematic analysis for this research study. This process was facilitated as a means of reflexivity to ascertain whether researcher bias and predispositions influenced data analysis. Colleagues were provided with and signed a confidentiality agreement (Appendix Q) reviewed the data collected, and thematic analysis processes, with no noteworthy feedback given. Although limited, these reflective approaches helped to ensure that this researcher did not view this research through a lens of solipsism. While the reflexivity exercises of this study may not be considered exhaustive and robust, it did provide opportunities for this researcher to self-examine. This sparsity of reflectivity and the approaches utilized can be considered a limitation of this study. This phenomenon will be explored further under the limitation section as noted in Chapter 5 of this study.

Data Analysis Steps

The data collected from participant responses were coded, grouped into categories and themes. They were subsequently extrapolated and amalgamated through thematic analysis to answer this study's research question. For this research study a determination was made to use an inductive process in coding, as opposed to a deductive approach. According to Kiger and Varpio (2020), an inductive method enables research findings to manifest in a generalized manner from the data collected without preconceived assumptions. Whereas, a deductive approach evokes a structured methodology (Judger, 2016), which includes preformulated ideas that can be contrasted alongside the data collected. This researcher wanted to ensure findings were data driven and that themes emerged independently without restraint from content derived from participants. (Dorsah & Okyer, 2020).

In an effort to answer the research question about the influence of self-care in the prevention of compassion fatigue in domestic violence advocates, a structured, systematic and progressive data analysis process was needed. As such, the framework utilized to facilitate thematic analysis for this research study manifested from six steps as outlined by Kiger and Varpio (2020) but developed by thematic analysis pioneering researchers, Braun and Clarke (2006). This six-step data analysis process included the following approaches. 1) The familiarization of the data 2) Generation of initial codes, 3) Search for themes, 4) Review of themes, 5) Defining and naming themes, 6) Production of the report. Considered an exemplary method of analysis, because of its ability to extrapolate from the data common patterns and shared meanings (Kiger & Varpio, 2020), these six steps were not meant to be rigidly linear (Majumdar, 2022) or strictly successive in nature but circuitous, with the researcher going back and forth as needed between steps, as the data is analyzed. Below are the six steps of thematic analysis utilized for this research study.

Step One: The familiarization of the Data

The commencement of data analysis utilizing the six-step data analysis (Kiger &Varpio, 2020, Braun & Clarke, 2006) required this researcher to become familiar with the data. The data set as provided by this qualitative descriptive study was derived from interviews and a focus group. This researcher read each transcript on multiple occasions to become familiar with the responses provided by participants, on average each transcript was read 6-7 times throughout the data analysis process. This step commenced when checking for accuracy while contrasting the video recording of interviews with transcripts, as provided by the voice-recognition software that transcribed the data. It was noted that the final transcript of interviews based on the voice recognition software, resulted in minor edits that had to be corrected by this researcher. Some words were inaccurately transcribed, minimal merging of the words of the interviewer and the interviewee, as well as correcting sentence structure. The process of listening and contrasting, helped this researcher become even more familiarized with the data and prepared for thematic analysis.

A total of thirteen (13) semi-structured interviews were conducted and one (1) focus group, were conducted for an estimated nine (9) hours of material collected. This initial reading enabled this researcher to become familiar with the data obtained which is considered a first and very important step in the thematic analysis process (Maguire & Delahunt, 2017). The initial reading of transcripts allowed this researcher to establish a cursory knowledge of the information shared, and become acquainted with the raw data, unencumbered of any preconceived notions or judgements. Appendix O provides a review of two (2) semi-structured interview transcripts.

Step Two: Generation of Initial Codes

After the initial reading of the data set, a more in-depth review of the transcripts was conducted, thematic analysis moved forward with the next step of generating codes using an inductive in vivo coding method. Using an in vivo coding approach enabled this researcher to utilize the exact words of participants (Rogers, 2018), as shared during interviews and the focus group. In vivo coding diminished researcher interpretation and allowed the voice of participants to be paramount throughout this study. **This inductive in vivo method provided the foundation needed to conduct data analysis enabling raw (Kiger & Varpio, 2020), interpretation of the data facilitated in an emergent manner.** For this research study, each step in establishing codes was progressive in nature and instrumental in producing the answer to the research question pertaining to the influence of self-care in the prevention of compassion fatigue. According to Kiger and Varpio (2020), codes can be considered the most simple and elementary manner in which to extrapolate meaning from raw data. The generation of codes for this study began with another review of transcripts. However, on this occasion of reading, intentionality and focus was placed on the responses of participants, as a cursory level of elucidation began to formalize. This researcher initially wrote notes in the margins of the transcripts beside responses or highlighted certain sections that were especially intriguing or noteworthy to the research question seeking to be answered. An example of the emergence of data coded can be found in interview question related to the type of self-care advocates engage in. Participants responses ranged from *sitting quietly* to taking a *nap* and *shopping.* In an inductive manner I would highlight each of these responses to ascertain if there was a pattern emerging from the data related to this research question. This intentional review of transcripts provided a high-level overview of participant responses and subsequent quotes and words that emerged were placed on a separate piece of paper. With this step, this researcher began the process of organizing the data and sections of the transcript were coded when it was determined to be germane and relevant in answering the research question (Maguire & Delahunt, 2017).

A representation of this process was captured when this researcher inquired with Participant #3, about **effective ways to prevent compassion fatigue.** Participant #3 shared "It's not always the big things. But I think most importantly, it's creating a foundation, where you know where to go for help for yourself, and being okay, with asking for help. This researcher was able to code this text as "asking for help". Similarly, when asked "what is your understanding of self-care" Participant #2 said, "allowing yourself to be vulnerable, knowing you have as much right to recuperate as the people you are helping", this statement was coded as "Advocate Rights". See Table 4 for a depiction of how codes were developed from participant responses.

Table 4

Example of the Development of Codes from Participant Responses

Participant	Interview Question	Interview Response	Code
3	Please share effective ways to prevent compassion fatigue?	"It's not always the big things. But I think most importantly, it's creating a foundation, where you know where to go for help for yourself, and being okay, with asking for help".	*Asking for help*
2	What is your understanding of self-care?	"Allowing yourself to be vulnerable, know you have as much right to recuperate as the people you are helping".	*Advocate Rights*

In an effort to capture and have organized the various codes progressively generated from the data, an initial listing of codes (Appendix M) was created. In addition, considered a catalogue of sorts, a codebook served as a foundational repository from which themes would eventually manifest (Braun, & Clarke, 2021). The codebook was beneficial to the data analysis process as it provided a classification system for the codes and the subsequent grouped categories which emerged from the data collected (Appendix N). This researcher was able to see patterns emerge from the data that were encapsulated as codes and placed in the codebook for closer review, evaluation, and alignment. After the initial round of coding was conducted, this researcher had captured 129 codes from the data collected as captured in the codebook. Through an iterative approach and further analysis, codes that were inter-related were grouped together, and were re-classified which encapsulated and summarized the totality of the group categories. This process was conducted through a thorough review of the codes, as similar codes were regrouped and classified, this merging and categorization setting the foundation for what would later develop into the formation of themes. Table # 5 provides an example of how codes became group categories which developed into categories along with a category description. Appendix N provides full review of the transition from code to group category and category. Table 5 provides an example of the development of codes, group categories and categories for this study.

Table 5

Example of Codes Development into Grouped Category and Category

Code	Grouped Category	Category	Description
Admitting when you are not the right person to help	Recognizing the tipping point, knowing yourself, asking for help	Self-Awareness	Advocates monitor their behavior and are conscientious about the use of self-care in preventing compassion fatigue.
Difficulty asking for help			
Don't have to be super advocate			
Recognize the signs of compassion fatigue			
Self-awareness			
Self-doubt			
Self-expression of frustration			
Self-neglect			
Self-preservation			
Self-reflection			
Superwoman/man cape			
The investment in self			
Time to be selfish			

Step Three: **Search for Themes**

In this step of thematic analysis efforts were placed on moving forward with locating themes from the data set. This researcher was required to continue the process of review, by re-reading each transcript. Doing so, created a level of familiarity providing the opportunity to group the established codes in an effort to progressively generate themes. Whereas the initial set of codes obtained did not have a structured format of categorization, a re-examination of the codes, enabled movement towards the refinement of the codes captured. For this step, in reviewing each code, this researcher removed those that were deemed redundant to the thematic analysis process.

During data collection participants would often share responses that were similar in nature and subsequently were grouped together. As patterns began to emerge, those codes that were similar in nature, were grouped together. An example of this process, related to responses pertaining to self-care, where advocates shared alike statements. In reference to interview questions about self-care, advocates shared that *self-care was unique* and that *self-care was individualized.* Each of these phrases shared the same meaning and presented data on the distinctive and personalized qualities that define self-care. Due to the similarities of these phrases, they were then merged into a group category entitled *type of self-care*.

Another example of similar phrases being merged manifested in response to advocates expressing how domestic violence is an unrelenting and on-going community issue. Advocates, stated that *domestic violence takes place 24/7*, that you *can't turn off domestic violence, no escape from domestic violence,* and clients experience *domestic violence crisis 24/7*. In merging these codes this researcher labeled them as this category b*oundaries* as the phenomenon of domestic violence permeated the lives of advocates without room to abscond their professional realm. Maguire and Delahunt (2017), report that there are no standardized and structured mandates with regards to the constitution and construct of a theme, but as they paint a broader story derived from the data, they should at a minimum be meaningful (Kiger & Varpio, 2020).

Step Three (3) in thematic analysis required a progressive approach to grouping compatible codes together, establishing a clear relationship between the codes delineated. In collecting data many participants spoke about the influence their self-care had on the domestic violence victims that they served. Participants spoke of *victim outcomes*; *quality vs quantity* and that *client(s) can tell when* (advocates) *not genuine self.* Each of these codes were grouped together as they were compatible with each other in relating to the influence of self-care on the victims' participants served. Subsequently, the broader category that manifested encapsulated each of these grouped categories and this category was aptly named, *victim impact.* Each group category transitioned into a category that was appropriately named to encapsulate a description of the codes and group categories combined. In the segue from code to group category to category, this researcher was intentional in ensuring each element progressed in answering this study's research question. Table six (6) provides an overview of how the grouped categories developed into the categories for this study.

Table 6

Group Category to Category

Group Category (Aligned Categories)	Category
Separation between work and personal life Intentionality	Boundaries
Recognizing tipping point Knowing yourself Asking for help	Self-Awareness
Supervisory support Advocate mentorship Agency self-care framework Healthy work environment Co-worker collaboration	Colleague/Organizational Care
Self-care impact on personal life Physical Health Mental Health	Holistic Well-being
Victim Outcomes Quality vs quantity	Victim Impact
Work outlook Career longevity Passion for advocacy	Career Longevity
Intentionality of self-care Frequency of self-care Type of self-care	Self-care Techniques

Step Four: Review of Themes

This step provided the opportunity for an additional layer of thematic analysis to be implemented. In the process of revealing the meaning behind this study, a higher level of categorization was utilized to highlight the themes emerged from the data collected in this study. This could only be achieved through the iterative process of reviewing the current categories this researcher had identified. Kiger and Varpio (2020), echo the thematic framework as established by Braun and Clarke (2006) in acknowledging that this step is critical in the fulfillment of thematic analysis. In this process, this researcher determined that the themes that emerged represented the codes, group categories and categories that became pronounced throughout thematic analysis. Appendix N provides a comprehensive presentation of this progressive process.

Group category such as the *Impact on Personal Life*, *Physical Health* and *Mental Health* were all placed under the category of *holistic well-being* which produced the following theme:

Domestic Violence Advocates take into consideration their holistic well-being in the prevention of compassion fatigue. This theme aptly reflected the comprehensive well-being of advocates and provided alignment with the codes, group category and category yielded by the data. As the development of themes continued, a stringent and iterative process of thematic review was adhered too. This phase helped to ensure that each theme was emblematic and supportive of the data captured (Kiger & Varpio, 2020) and comprehensively coded. Table 7 provides an example of the incremental process from interview question to the development of a theme.

Table 7

Development of Theme from Research Question, Code to Category

Research Question	Interview Question	Direct Quote	Code	Category	Theme
RQ2: How do domestic violence advocates from the Mid-Atlantic region of the United States use self-care to prevent compassion fatigue?	Q#8. Please describe your motivation for using self-care techniques?	P#3. *I want to continue being in the field so that one day domestic violence won't be so bad.*	Diminish domestic violence	Career longevity	Domestic Violence Advocates utilize self-care activities to maintain the quality of their professional life and help prevent compassion fatigue.
		P#10. *I want to be in industry long-term, to prevent depression and anxiety from creeping up.*	Develop as an advocate		
		P#6: *To be at our best for the people and the clientele to get them the help they need.*	Best that I can be		

Step Five: Defining and Naming Themes

In this step, the theme evaluative process continued, with a refined focus on explaining the phenomenon being studied (Ozuem, Willis & Howell, 2022). While this stage symbolized the near completion of thematic analysis, this researcher iteratively and intermittently reverted to previous steps to further solidify accuracy of analysis and categorization. The process of defining and naming the developed themes, enabled this researcher to "hone in on the most important aspect of each theme" (Kiger & Varpio, 2020 p.7). With this heightened level of synthesis, each theme was concisely and clearly defined to encapsulate the meaning of the theme. The theme was then broadly classified with a descriptive value attached and labeled for categorization. Through the iterative process, this researcher ensured that the definition and theme names were in alignment with each designated theme, derived throughout the thematic analysis process. From the raw data, thematic analysis commenced with originating codes, progressing towards categories. Duplicate coded data were removed, and pattern interpretation took place which resulted in the emergence of themes. An example of this process is found in the category labeled, *Colleague/Organizational Leadership*. This category encapsulated codes wherein respondents spoke of the influence of their colleagues and supervisory leadership as it related to their self-care and prevention of compassion fatigue. The data obtained in relation to this theme highlighted the important role that coworkers and supervisors played in providing accountability and setting the tone for self-care. Patterns of data surrounding this theme figured prominently throughout the data collected. As such the theme was aptly named *Domestic Violence Advocates utilize their colleagues and organizational leadership for support and accountability in the prevention of compassion fatigue*. The named theme fully encapsulated and described the coded data. Each theme was named and defined in alignment with this study's two (2) research questions. Table 8 provides an overview of this study's named themes that manifested through thematic analysis.

Table 8

Named Themes

Theme #	Themes
Theme 1.	Domestic Violence Advocates intentionally create boundaries between their work and personal life in order to prevent compassion fatigue.
Theme 2.	Domestic Violence Advocates use self-awareness as a self-care technique in the prevention of compassion fatigue.
Theme 3.	Domestic Violence Advocates utilize their colleagues and organizational leadership for support and accountability in the prevention of compassion fatigue.
Theme 4.	Domestic Violence Advocates take their holistic well-being into consideration in the prevention of compassion fatigue.
Theme 5.	Domestic violence Advocates utilize therapeutic strategies to prevent compassion fatigue in order to have a positive influence on the victims they serve.
Theme 6.	Domestic Violence Advocates utilize assorted self-care activities to ensure they maintain the longevity and quality of their professional life and prevent compassion fatigue.
Theme 7.	Domestic Violence advocates engage in assorted therapeutic activities to prevent compassion fatigue.

Step Six: Production of the Report

While this step marked the final phase in data analysis, this researcher in a peripheral manner, continued the repetitive process denoted in steps 1-5 (Kiger & Varpio, 2020), while compiling this study's findings. The written report provides a comprehensive chronology of data analysis from inception to conclusive findings. Through a detailed report, this researcher was able to share the story of this study in narrative form, as derived from the raw data, obtained in data collection. Each theme was elaborated upon in the report to include rich detail, participant direct quotes examples, demonstrating a distinct correlation and validity between the data, and the subsequent themes emerged from data analysis (Nowell, Norris, White & Moules, 2017). In writing this report, this researcher ensured that the themes that emerged were juxtaposed and aligned to expound upon the influence of self-care in the prevention of compassion fatigue in domestic violence advocates.

Trustworthiness

In an effort to establish trustworthiness in this qualitative descriptive study, it was essential to demonstrate elements of rigor, to ensure confidence in the synthesized data collected, analyzed and the subsequent results. Several elements were utilized to solidify trustworthiness of this study, such as convening an expert panel, field testing, member checking and the use of a structured interview protocol. An exhaustive search was conducted, and three (3) researchers were selected to utilize the Validation Rubric for Expert Panel (White & Simon, 2019), to vet the questions that were compiled to answer the research question for this study. Expert panelists were qualitative researchers or subject matter expert professionals with terminal degrees. Expert panelist recommendations were adhered to, and domestic violence advocates who were not part of this study, were interviewed for field testing purposes. The data from these interviews were transcribed and field testers provided salient feedback on the interview questions asked of them. It is important to note that data collected from field testing was not incorporated in the results of this study. Upon completion of interviews and a focus group, this data was transcribed and returned to participants for member checking purposes. While participants returned the transcripts with edits as deemed appropriate, this researcher did not provide a summary of interpreted data, and this is a limitation towards trustworthiness that is explored in Chapter 5. This researcher incorporated reflexivity as a means of trustworthiness, to help ensure that bias and subjectivity did not permeate the data analysis process. In addition, to solidify dependability and confirmability, methodical documentation of study details was facilitated throughout the research process to have a record of study processes. An interview protocol (Appendix I) was also included to support research transferability. Data analysis was also conducted in a chronological and simplified manner using Kiger and Varpio (2020), to support reliability and trustworthiness (Elo et al. (2014).

Results

Presenting the Results

The results section of this qualitative descriptive study captures the multiple themes that emerged from thematic analysis. This data was obtained through semi-structured interviewed and a focus group wherein domestic violence advocates from the Mid-Atlantic region of the United States, were queried about the influence of self-care in the prevention of compassion fatigue. As addressed previously in this chapter, data saturation was achieved when no new data emerged from the data collected. This researcher systematically analyzed this data, enabling codes to become grouped categories, which evolved into categories to themes. Throughout this process marginal reflexivity was exercised, to distinguish between this researchers' preconceptions and study participants lived experiences and meaning in response to the research questions. The reflexivity practice of this researcher throughout data analysis, could be considered a limitation of this study, and is further expounded upon in Chapter 5. Throughout this process seven (7) themes manifested to answer the research questions as delineated by this study. In an effort to answer each research question, synthesis of the data occurred, and the themes are presented in the following results section. Table 9 presents an overview of the themes extrapolated from the data collected in response to the research questions of this study.

Table 9

Summary of Group Category, Category and Themes by Research Question

Research Question	Group Category	Category	Theme
RQ1: What self-care techniques do domestic violence advocates from the Mid-Atlantic region of the United States describe as typically being used in the prevention of compassion fatigue?	Separation between work and personal life, intentionality	Boundaries	Domestic Violence Advocates intentionally create boundaries between their work and personal life in order to prevent compassion fatigue.
	Recognizing tipping point, Knowing yourself, asking for help	Self-Awareness	Domestic Violence Advocates use self-awareness as a self-care technique in the prevention of compassion fatigue.
	Supervisory support, Advocate mentorship, Agency self-care framework, Healthy work environment, Co-worker collaboration	Colleagues/Organizational Leadership	Domestic Violence Advocates utilize their colleagues and organizational leadership for support and accountability in the prevention of compassion fatigue.
	Self-care impact on personal life, Physical health, Mental health	Holistic Well-being	Domestic Violence Advocates take their holistic well-being into consideration in the prevention of compassion fatigue.
RQ2: How do domestic violence advocates from the Mid-Atlantic region of the United States use self-care to prevent compassion fatigue?	Victim Outcomes, quality vs quantity	Victim Impact	Domestic violence Advocates utilize therapeutic strategies to prevent compassion fatigue in order to have a positive influence on the victims they serve.
	Work outlook, career longevity, passion for advocacy	Career Longevity	Domestic Violence Advocates utilize assorted self-care activities to ensure they maintain the longevity and quality of their professional life and prevent compassion fatigue.
	Frequency of Self-care, Intentionality of Self-care, Type of Self-care	Self-care Techniques	Domestic violence advocates engage in assorted therapeutic activities to prevent compassion fatigue.

Research Question 1

What self-care techniques do domestic violence advocates from the Mid-Atlantic region of the United States describe as typically being used in the prevention of compassion fatigue? To answer this research question participants engaged in semi-structured interviews and a focus group. Participants who engaged in the semi-structured interviews were not the same participants in the focus group. Subsequently, all participants were asked the same interview questions with the goal of answering the overarching research question for this study. As a foundational question for this study, research question one (1) sought to explore and elucidate self-care techniques utilized by advocates. As domestic violence advocates are exposed to the trauma experienced by the victims they serve, self-care is considered an essential tool in helping to prevent compassion fatigue from derailing professional expectations and responsibilities. Study participants in the semi-structured interviews and the focus group, shared their experiences and their rich descriptions helped to bring forth the themes that answered this research question one (1). Through coding, categories and the resulting emerging themes, four themes manifested from responses garnered from the semi-structured interviews and focus group. Table 8 provides the themes for this research question.

Table 10

RQ1 Themes

Research Questions	Themes
RQ1: What self-care techniques do domestic violence advocates from the Mid-Atlantic region of the United States describe as typically being used in the prevention of compassion fatigue?	Theme 1 Domestic Violence Advocates intentionally create boundaries between their work and personal life in order to prevent compassion fatigue. Theme 2 Domestic Violence Advocates use self-awareness as a self-care technique in the prevention of compassion fatigue. Theme 3 Domestic Violence Advocates utilize their colleagues and organizational leadership for support and accountability in the prevention of compassion fatigue. Theme 4 Domestic Violence Advocates take their holistic well-being into consideration in the prevention of compassion fatigue.

Theme 1: Domestic Violence Advocates Intentionally Create Boundaries Between their Work and Personal Life in order to Prevent Compassion Fatigue.

This theme described the importance of establishing clearly defined lines between domestic violence advocacy and the personal lives of advocates. Participants described the challenges related to achieving and maintaining boundaries, in the realm of their work and personal life. The detriment of not clearly delineating between the two, impacted the prevention of compassion fatigue. Advocates often found it difficult to leave work behind and would carry work assignments with them beyond the scope of their work hours, which aligns with the literature on this subject (Logan & Walker, 2018). Participants spoke freely that crossing boundaries often served as a gateway to compassion fatigue and how challenging it is to set aside this work. Participants shared that establishing boundaries would often evoke feelings of selfishness, for placing their needs before the needs of the victims they served. In response to this research question, advocates described that when there are no boundaries, it is easily demonstrated in diminished work-life balance. Other advocates become keenly aware of their colleagues' poor boundaries as shared by Participant # 1 who said, "I can tell in the practices like what time they send their emails that they are not cutting it off and knowing what your particular limits are because you just can't do everything". P#4 echoed the importance of having boundaries in this line of work, "You have to disconnect, you have to be able to at some point to put this work down and focus and as selfish as that sounds you have to focus on yourself. P#5 shared a personal experience when poor boundaries were explained to a victim, "God bless this client, because I had to explain to her that I'm probably the only person in the agency who is going to answer the phone on a Sunday". In contrast, strict and rigid boundaries as part of self-care can have a specific framework as shared by P#9: "healthy boundaries would look like if you're off of work, you're off of work, and don't exceed that time", similarly P#2 shared that "When you get that compassion fatigue that you start crossing boundaries. When you go to work, brush your home life off and when you leave work brush your work life off.

> P#11: having like a really good work life balance is helpful…. you know, it's the little things like that, that you don't realize what a toll they take after until it's been like three weeks that I'm working late on a Friday. And then I'm wondering why I'm so annoyed. So I try to like, really get that stuff in balance as fast as I can before I start getting resentful about all the extra work. So, I think having like a work life balance, in that sense, making sure that I am able to go for a walk during the day, especially with work from

home, like being able to, like take some time to just like, move, or even just like, not look at my email while I eat lunch. Even if that's for 15 minutes, you know, I took email notifications off my phone, which has like, changed my life. Because now I check email, like it's still every hour or so. But I don't feel like I'm bombarded with it. I can sort of control when the chaos comes to me.

In describing boundaries as part of their self-care technique, P#3 stated that "It took me so long to learn to create boundaries between work and home". The theme of boundaries as described by advocates is considered essential in the use of self-care in the prevention of compassion fatigue and is often utilized as a best practice. A total of thirty (30) codes emerged from the data in support of this theme which represented 13.17% of the total codes from this study (Appendix N). This led to two (2) categories a) separation between work and personal life and the implementation of b) intentionality in preventing compassion fatigue and addressing self-care. This data led to the theme that domestic violence advocates intentionally create boundaries between their work and personal life in order to prevent compassion fatigue. The data collected to include codes and categories and resulting theme, helped to support and answer research question one (1).

Theme 2. Domestic Violence Advocates Use Self-Awareness as a Self-Care Technique in the Prevention of Compassion Fatigue. Participants described the key role that self-awareness plays in the prevention of compassion fatigue and as a strategy of self-care. The inability to self-reflect and gauge current standings as it relates to self-care, provides a platform for compassion fatigue to emerge. The category groups, of a) knowing yourself, b) recognizing your tipping point and c) knowing when to ask for help, all relate to internal processes that promote the theme of self-awareness in answering research question one. Participants shared that Advocates should be aware of the importance of knowing when to administer self-care. This theme as espoused by participants is deemed critical in the prevention of compassion fatigue, as self-awareness provided the internal motivation needed to engage in self-care.

Understanding about compassion fatigue was determined important in helping to prevent it from consuming advocates. Additionally, participants shared that without this self-awareness they would not know when it was time to ask for help from colleagues or organizational leaders. In addition, throughout data analysis this researcher observed as described in the data, participants giving themselves consent to ask for assistance as a means of preventing compassion fatigue. Without this self-awareness, participants began to question why they were in this field, while sharing the importance of learning about themselves as a means for self-care. Stilos and Wynnychuk (2021), report that self-care can be enhanced when there is self-awareness, which can produce positive outcomes. Self-care can best be deployed when you know yourself, this theme was supported by P#5 who described it as, "knowing when I need a break", and P#4 echoed this sentiment by stating in the semi-structured interview that "I'm very in touch with myself and knowing when I need to take a break". Participant #6 shared that "Knowing that it exists, I'm determined to prevent it, motivates me to make sure I'm filling my cup". Advocates highlighted the need to recognize when they came to a tipping point of being overwhelmed with service delivery and acknowledged how and when they needed to ask for help. P#10 describes this phenomenon by stating that,

> If you don't practice that self-awareness, then, you know, those, like depression and anxious symptoms, they can creep up on you. You know, before you know it, it's just like, why am I angry? Like, why am I not believing the client as much as I would normally do? Like, why am I not practicing trauma informed approaches that I've been taught?

Part of self-awareness is understanding when to ask for help which often comes from fellow advocates and to get tasks completed. "Creating a foundation, where you know where to go for help for yourself and being okay with asking for help" says P#3. A total of thirteen (13) codes emerged from the data in support of this theme which represented 10.06% of the data collected (Appendix N). This led to three (3) categories, a) knowing yourself, b) recognizing your tipping point and c) knowing when to ask for help. These categories developed into the theme that domestic violence advocates use self-awareness as a self-care technique in the prevention of compassion fatigue. The codes and categories that emerged from the data supported this theme in answering research question one (1).

Theme 3: Domestic Violence Advocates Utilize their Colleagues and Organizational Leadership for Support and Accountability in the Prevention of Compassion Fatigue. Theme 3 provided support in answering research question one (1) by describing the role that colleagues and organizational leadership plays in the prevention of compassion fatigue. The categories that supported this theme included a) supervisory support, b) advocate mentorship, c) agency self-care framework d) a healthy work environment and e) co-worker collaboration. Responses to this research question described how participants often sought out organizational leadership to set the tone for participants self-care, while leaning on team members for accountability and support. The support from colleagues and organizational leadership was considered a major theme in response to preventing compassion fatigue and practicing self-care. Many advocates affirmed the role of their supervisor in establishing self-care as a priority and whether they received support when seeking to engage in self-care. Participants shared about having quarterly self-care events, staff retreats, creating a safe space environment, and the importance of leadership flexibility, which were all coded and grouped under the theme of colleague/organizational care. In addition, participants noted that a toxic work environment played a role in advocate affect, and subsequent compassion fatigue. Most of the participants spoke of their work environment and described organizations that would often tout the importance of self-care yet were not intentional and practical in the implementation of such strategies. Throughout interviews and the focus group, this researcher observed an informal mentorship taking place as participants described the relationship between novice and seasoned advocates in the encouragement of self-care. In response to how self-care influences the prevention of compassion fatigue P#8 shared that within their organization

> Having a mentor…. and our Executive Director…they're able to help me be mindful that, okay it might be time for you to take a day off… I will say that I didn't recognize that I was getting to that point of compassion fatigue.

Fellow advocates can see the compassion fatigue in other advocates and can point out when self-care is needed. As P#17 shares, "we know if someone's not together right now and they need help we know that we can call on our team to help us out and pull the weight while we're taking care of other things". Likewise, P#7 shares how at their organization you can "Just talk it over with another staff member might be able to bring perspective by asking questions to see if you did what you were supposed to do or not and remind each other to take deep breaths and collect ourselves". In contrast P# 4 shares that, "I feel like many people wouldn't tell their boss, I just need a mental health day, because it's a reflection on you, like you can't keep up and do what you're supposed to do". In the prevention of compassion fatigue having a healthy work environment that supports advocates usage of self-care is the responsibility of all from executive leadership who set the tone, to front-line advocates who practice self-care. In addition, collaboration takes place as seasoned advocates mentor new advocates by modeling self-care, and there is transparency amongst advocates that can positively influence the work environment.

The data for this theme was supported by twenty-six (26) codes which comprised 20.13% of the data collected (Appendix N) for this study. This led to five (5) categories that supported this theme which included a) supervisory support, b) advocate mentorship, c) agency self-care framework d) a healthy work environment and e) co-worker collaboration. These categories helped to solidify the theme that domestic violence advocates utilize their colleagues and organizational leadership for support and accountability, in the prevention of compassion fatigue. The data collected from this study and the resulting theme, helped to support and answer research question one (1).

Theme 4. Domestic Violence Advocates Take Their Holistic Well-Being into Consideration in the Prevention of Compassion Fatigue. The emphasis of this theme reflected how participants described the influence of compassion fatigue and self-care on them mentally, physically, and personally. Multiple codes highlighted the importance of this theme and the importance of comprehensively addressing all elements of the participants lives. Some of the categories that supported this theme included a) self-care impact on personal life, b) physical health, c) mental health. Throughout this theme participants recognized the positive benefits of self-care on their families and shared the negative influence on their families when self-care is neglected. Many participants shared how the exposure to victim trauma resulted in a psychological toll, such as feeling numb, drained, and wiped out. In addition to physical impact, participants also shared the psychological influence they experienced describing it as an emotional liability if self-care is not appropriately addressed. These physical and mental descriptions were then coded and grouped together and amalgamated under this theme. In addition, participants spoke of the social aspects of self-care and being known as an advocate in the community. Many shared being called to help a victim on days off, in social settings and how this position provides little reprieve when participants seek to remain balanced and address their total care. Maintaining advocate mental health and family wellbeing was also considered a key factor in the prevention of compassion fatigue. P#4 who said,

> I need to be mentally healthy. I don't want to dread going to work. So, to combat that, I'm finding ways to you know, keep me mentally well, and then of course, my family like I just feel like it's a domino effect. If you don't take care of your mind, then it just starts to spiral out of control.

P#5 spoke of the physical and mental rational behind the use of self-care.

I don't want to drop dead of heart attack at 50 I'll be honest. So, my motivation is really to make sure I stay healthy enough to continue. I don't want to ever reach burnout. I know the statistics for burnout, in this field and they are very very high. I don't want my boss to have to come tell me I need to take time off. Because maybe and then have to question Is it something other than you know, what am I am I not doing something in my job? Or am I just looking so stressed to them? That, you know, I am carrying it over in my work.

Not only does compassion fatigue influence their work but participants also noted how it impacts their family and home life. P#7 shared, "This can manifest in different ways, one of the ways is lashing out not necessarily at the person that you're helping, but you would go home and lash out to your family members, and they're looking at you like, what is wrong with you? I come home and I try not to let out my feelings, but sometimes it does come out". P#12 also described how compassion fatigue influences their family "wanting to respect my family, in that I am not allowing myself to be fatigued and stressed and irritable, because that is definitely not fair to them. So, I want to definitely value them and respect them, and not bring all of that to the table when I come home. I want home to be home. And I want it to be a place of peace and relaxation". The descriptions provided by participants provided rich detail in demonstrating augmenting how this theme addresses their holistic wellbeing.

The data for this theme was supported by twenty-one (1) codes which comprised 16.27% of the data collected (Appendix N) for this study. This led to three (3) categories that supported this theme which included a) self-care impact on personal life, b) physical health, c) mental health. These categories helped to support the theme that domestic violence advocates take their holistic well-being into consideration in the prevention of compassion fatigue. The data collected from this study along with the codes and categories that developed into this theme, helped to support and answer research question one (1).

Research Question 1 Conclusion. The first research question for this study sought to gain understanding in response to what self-care techniques do domestic violence advocates describe as typically being used in the prevention of compassion fatigue? A total of ninety (90) codes contributed to the development of this theme. With thirteen (13) category groups, and four (4) categories emerging in support of the four (4) themes that answered research question one. Rich descriptions were yielded by participants who shared their perspectives resulting in four (4) themes manifesting from the data. The first theme related to boundaries, and participants shared about the maintenance of work-life balance and communicated about intentionality in implementing limitations to prevent compassion fatigue. Within this theme, participants also spoke of observing inadequate self-care practices in their colleagues and the tell-tale signs of their disengagement, and how easily this can result in compassion fatigue. In the second theme participants provided insight into self-awareness as means of mitigating compassion fatigue and embracing self-care. From being able to recognize when assistance and colleague support is needed, to participants paying attention to their internal indicators, self-care was described as maintainable. The third theme that manifested from the data collected focused on the role of colleagues and organizational support to aid in the prevention of compassion fatigue. A majority of participants shared how essential leadership edict on self-care was to their own maintenance of self-care, and how colleagues may support this effort. Within the fourth theme, participants addressed their holistic wellbeing as a contributing factor to their self-care. Some advocates shared the toll advocacy had on their physical being and comprehensive welfare. Insight gleaned from participants in response to research question one (1), provided depth and results as it relates to advocates and the influence of self-care in the prevention of compassion fatigue.

Research Question 2

How do domestic violence advocates from the Mid-Atlantic region of the United States use self-care to prevent compassion fatigue? Research question 2 (two) provided the opportunity for participants of this study to describe the practical principles that govern their self-care and in doing so how it counteracts and diminishes participant compassion fatigue. To extrapolate such rich descriptions the use of semi-structured interviews and a focus group were utilized as data collection methods. Carefully crafted and thoroughly vetted questions were compiled to ensure that research question two (2) produced responses that answered this study's overarching research question. From this research question three (3) themes originated. Table 9 provides an overview of the themes for this research question.

Table 11

RQ2. Themes

Research Question	Themes
RQ2: How do domestic violence advocates from the Mid-Atlantic region of the United States use self-care to prevent compassion fatigue?	Theme 5 Domestic violence Advocates utilize therapeutic strategies to prevent compassion fatigue in order to have a positive influence on the victims they serve. Theme 6 Domestic Violence Advocates utilize assorted self-care activities to ensure they maintain the longevity and quality of their professional life and prevent compassion fatigue. Theme 7 Domestic violence Advocates engage in assorted therapeutic activities to prevent compassion fatigue.

Each of these themes encapsulated the answers to this research question. This researcher was able to observe as many participants spoke of their desire to help victims of domestic violence as motivation for self-care, while others shared their motivation for professional longevity as a rationale to prevent compassion fatigue. The additional theme that arose from this research question centered on the myriad of self-care techniques used by advocates, in the prevention of compassion fatigue. The semi-structured interviews and focus group provided the most apropos data collection to in which to obtain the responses needed to answer this research question.

Theme 5: Domestic violence Advocates utilize therapeutic strategies to prevent compassion fatigue in order to have a positive influence on the victims they serve.

This theme related to the emphasis participants placed on those they were meant to serve, the victims of domestic violence. Multiple codes supported the development of this theme. The categories supporting this theme were a) victim outcomes and b) quality vs quantity. At the crux of participant engagement in self-care was the influence it had on the fragile population of clients they worked for. Intentionality with self-care served as a positive reinforcement as it yielded better results for participants and victims of domestic violence. Participants also transparently shared the negative impact their inability to achieve self-care had on them and victims. This theme depicted participants investment in self-care as a commitment to the empowerment and wellbeing of victims. In response to this research question participants described self-care as a meant to prevent compassion fatigue so that they may have a positive influence on the victims they serve.

When participants were asked the effect that self-care has on advocates, participants described that it fostered resiliency, mental clarity and bolstered confidence, which were all attributes that serve to benefit the victims served. Many participants expressed their desire to help diminish the cycle of violence victims faced and espoused the quality of service provided as a direct benefit of self-care intentionality. A concentric view of this phenomenon was provided by P#15 who shared that "self-care is part of community care and community care is part of anti-violence work, so self-care is doing our work". Likewise, P#2 said, "If I'm not healthy how can I help them (victims) to become heathy". Participants shared how their self-care corelates to the quality of services received by victims of domestic violence. This thought was supported by P#9 who said, "If you're not doing any self-care, you're not going to be able to invest your time in your clients or it could be the opposite effect, where you're going to be so overwhelmed that you have it. This statement was also shared by P#19 who said self-care "corelates with the quality of work that you're able to give back to clients". Participants were also keen on how their lack of self-care may deter victims from communicating their needs with their advocate. According to P#10,

> With clients, you know, if you're not taking care of yourself, it can have a negative effect on them. Because you may not be willing to offer them your best in terms of like your work. And, you know, they may pick up on that vibe that you know, you're upset, and they just don't come to you and talk to you about what they need to because they're worried about you instead of them. And dv victims are very compassionate people. So, they will often, you know, try to talk to you about your problems instead of their own.

Along with this statement pertaining to the theme of advocates self-care influence on victims, P#14 shared how advocates, "Can't be efficient…if you're running on empty" and P#5 expressed that "It can be difficult to separate and take care of yourself because you feel that one time that I'm not going to be there then that would be someone's life". The data also revealed the importance of advocates regularly engaging in self-care to not experience compassion fatigue, and to model appropriate behavior for victims.

P#10 "It's something that you really have to watch out for, and you have to manage your self-care on a regular basis, so it doesn't creep up on you. Because before I knew what compassion fatigue was, and I was working in the shelter, I got to a point where I just felt like it wasn't the field for me. And I almost ended up, you know, quitting and taking a job in like the financial industry instead, because I thought, you know, maybe trauma is not for me, because I wasn't talking about it with anybody. I wasn't, you know, practicing my self-care actively, like I should, but I was, you know, teaching shelter clients to do so. So, I wasn't taking my own advice".

The data for this theme was supported by fifteen (15) codes which comprised 11.62% of the data collected (Appendix N) for this study. This led to two (2) categories, a) victim outcomes and b) quality vs quantity. These categories helped to support the theme that Domestic violence Advocates utilize therapeutic strategies to prevent compassion fatigue in order to have a positive influence on the victims they serve.

The data collected from this study through the codes and categories that developed into this theme, helped to support and answer research question two (2).

Theme 6. Domestic Violence Advocates Utilize Assorted Self-Care Activities to Ensure They Maintain the Longevity and Quality of Their Professional Life and Prevent Compassion Fatigue. The data that produced this theme revealed the commitment that participants had to this professional field and ultimately the service to victims of domestic violence. The categories supporting this theme included a) work outlook, b) career longevity and c) passion for advocacy. In response to this research question participants shared their strong desire to remain long-term in the field of advocacy, and to do so, determined that self-care must regularly be deployed. Their professional longevity would need to be one of quality as participants sought to make the lives of their client victims better. In recognizing the cost of caring (Figley, 2017) participants often weighed the ever-increasing demand of the profession with the innate exposure to the traumas of the victim served, and how best to balance each of these elements.

Participants expressed being cognizant of the probable exposure to compassion fatigue while in this field, and the importance of self-care, yet proffered not deploying self-care strategies on a regular basis. Sufficient data was provided for this theme as responses corelated with this research question as participants use their motivation to have a quality professional life to prevent compassion fatigue. This theme also presented personal motivations for engaging in quality professional work, due to many participants being survivors of domestic violence and wanting to provide for others the quality support they themselves received at one point from an advocate. Participants shared the importance of having a quality professional experience based on the gravity of the life-saving work being facilitated on the behalf of victims of domestic violence.

The data also revealed participant work ethic in this field and a need for more self-care. P#8 said "Especially within this work, a lot of us become Workaholics. We put in a lot a lot of time within the work and so, I'm not going to say that we don't practice self-care, we could do better. I'll be honest with saying that practicing self-care more often wouldn't hurt". P#4 expressed similar viewpoints, "I think that the advocates, maybe not all, I can't speak for all, and this is just my perspective, but I think that the advocates believe that the more they do, the more productive they seem. That is a problem with capitalistic society. Because I don't think that because you're working at seven o'clock at night, you're being more productive. That's not my view of it, I think that you are overcompensating, and I think you need to cut it off". With regards to the longevity of professional experience, P#3 said "I want to keep being in this field", while P#1 shared, "If you don't take care of yourself or if you don't feel like you deserve to take care of yourself then I don't think this is something that you would be in for long-term. P#6 described a broader and more personal objective stating that "I am survivor of domestic violence, so I believe that fuels my passion to be the best advocate that I can for anyone and everyone's whos' struggling with domestic violence". P#13 detailed the importance of self-care in the prevention of compassion fatigue and described the influence on domestic violence advocates;

> I've had someone say, you know, I don't experience compassion fatigue, like, it's a bad thing, you know, and it's not that it's a bad thing. This is just part of what happens when we do this job. 100% It almost has the same stigma of mental illness. I will talk about self-care for hours, because it's so important especially for domestic violence work, it's the most important thing, because you will get burnt out in a week if you don't do something.

The data for this theme was supported by seven (7) codes which comprised 5.32% of the data collected (Appendix N) for this study. This led to three (3) categories, a) work outlook, b) career longevity and c) passion for advocacy. These categories helped to support the theme that domestic violence advocates utilize assorted self-care activities to ensure they maintain the longevity and quality of their professional life and prevent compassion fatigue, which answered research question two (2).

Theme 7. Domestic Violence Advocates Engage in Assorted Therapeutic Activities to Prevent Compassion Fatigue. Participants shared numerous self-care techniques utilized as they sought to prevent compassion fatigue and revealed a need for advocates to engage in self-care more proactively. The grouped categories that supported this theme are a) intentionality of self-care, b) frequency of self-care, and c)- Type of self-care. Participants connected that they must regularly and intentionally implement self-care strategies in an effort to diminish the effects of compassion fatigue. In response to this research question, participants were able to share the most influential self-care strategy utilized in prevention of compassion fatigue. Responses from participants yielded a vast description of self-care strategies that ranged from the engagement in physical movement, mental regulation, and spiritual enlightenment activities.

The data demonstrated an assortment of self-care techniques that advocates use to prevent compassion fatigue, such as their faith, exercise, deep breathing, meditating, exercising, and even humor as a tool to self-regulate. Participants descriptions of self-care strategies demonstrated their awareness and importance of incorporating these approaches on a regular basis as a best practice of self-care. In addition, this theme is in alignment with the research question as it highlights the plethora of self-care techniques participants described utilizing as they seek to prevent compassion fatigue. In reference to how regularly advocates use self-care, the data revealed not as often, P#6 said "there is a tendency to not regularly engage in self-care", likewise P#7 stated, "I can't speak for anybody else; I can only speak for myself. I don't do it as much as I can or should".

Participants shared the resource that therapeutic engagement is as a form of self-care in addressing mental well-being. P#3 said "we tell our survivors hey you should go to therapy for all this trauma you're experiencing. Hey, maybe I should too, you know, that honestly, its helpers need help, too". Intentionality of spiritual belief and faith was interwoven as a self-care technique as described by some participants. P#6, described the core value of faith in response to this research question, stating that "For me it's my Faith, God put me on this path of being an advocate, so it's a calling, so He equipped me, and so therefore He's given me this position and I'm just doing the best that I know through self-care methods, which is praise and worship through Him in prayer".

In addition, establishing boundaries, learning to delegate, and asking for help were also shared as self-care strategies. P#8 shared a unique and symbolic self-care strategy that learned from another care professional "I learned from my niece who is a psychologist and she said that one of the things that she learns to do after she sees her clients is she forces herself to get up and go wash her hands and that before she leaves the office every day she washes her hands as a reminder to wash it off and to let it go and so I thought that was really interesting. So, I definitely have been doing more of that". As described and expounded upon through the data, participants connected in this theme, that they must regularly and intentionally implement self-care strategies in an effort to diminish the effects of compassion fatigue.

The data for this theme was supported by seventeen (17) codes which comprised 13.17% of the data collected (Appendix N) for this study. This led to three (3) categories, a a) intentionality of self-care, b) frequency of self-care, and c) type of self-care. These categories helped to support the theme that domestic violence advocates engage in assorted therapeutic activities to prevent compassion fatigue. The data collected from this study through the codes and categories produced the resulting theme, which helped to support and answer research question two (2).

Research Question 2 Conclusion. The purpose of this research was to describe how domestic violence advocates use self-care to prevent compassion fatigue. Based on responses obtained from the semi-structured interviews and focus group as evidenced through data saturation, three (3) themes emerged from the data, Domestic Violence

Advocates use self-awareness as a self-care technique in the prevention of compassion fatigue, Domestic Violence Advocates utilize their colleagues and organizational leadership for support and accountability in the prevention of compassion fatigue and Domestic Violence Advocates engage in assorted therapeutic activities to prevent compassion fatigue. A total of thirty ninety (39) codes contributed to the development of this theme. With eight (8) categories group together resulting in three (3) categories emerging in support of the three (3) themes that answered research question two.

Participants discussed the influence their self-care had on the victims they served. Lack of self-care produced a deleterious effect on victims, whereas a robust self-care regiment provided a beneficial effect on victims, as described by study participants. In response to this research question, most participants expressed their commitment to remaining in this professional field and provide quality services to victims as a means toward achieving their self-care and compassion fatigue prevention. Through the data captured in response to this research question, participants were able to expound upon and describe the assorted self-care strategies utilized in the maintenance of their well-being.

Reflexivity Based on Thematic Analysis

Throughout data analysis and the emergence of themes, elements of reflexivity were incorporated to assess researcher subjectivity. Treharne and Riggs (2014), discuss the importance of researchers reflecting inwardly about their influence on thematic analysis. This researcher sought to be aware of any preconceptions that may have unduly biased the results of this study. While a formally documented reflexivity protocol such as reflexive journaling and bracketing were not conducted, personal and peer reflexivity were implemented. Throughout the progressive phases of data analysis this researcher would institute intentionality and pause at each phase to reflect inwardly. This approach enabled the researcher at intermittent intersections to examine the data and ascertain whether there was any researcher influence introduced in analysis. This cognitive approach provided the opportunity to distinguish between participant responses and perceptions, and that of this researcher's ideology and preconceived notions about the data. This iterative process provided this researcher the ability to demonstrate high-level conscientiousness in ensuring bias was diminished, which enabled a deeper understanding of participant perspective to manifest. In addition, throughout the research process, peer reflexivity was utilized by reflecting with colleagues who work within the field, of this subject matter. In doing so, invaluable feedback was provided which enabled additional support in this researcher's efforts to be self-evaluative. It is noteworthy, that this exercise in reflexivity was facilitated in an informal manner and as such, could be considered a limitation and a barrier to complete trustworthiness of this study. This limitation is further expounded upon in Chapter 5, strengths and weaknesses of this study.

Summary

In summary, Chapter 4 consisted of relaying findings found in this study and the process utilized to obtain these results, from data collection to data analysis. The underlying question this research sought to answer related to the influence of self-care in the prevention of compassion fatigue in domestic violence advocates. Chapter 4 included descriptive statistics, the role of the expert panel, field testing and member checking in solidifying trustworthiness. A qualitative descriptive approach was utilized along with interviews and a focus group, as data collection sources. The sample population for this study included nineteen (19) participants who were domestic violence advocates, over the age of 18 years old, employed at domestic violence organization, within the Mid-Atlantic region of the United States. Thirteen (13) participants engaged in semi-structured interviews and six (6) participants were part of the focus group conducted for this study. Interviews ranged from 18 minutes to 59 minutes, with an average length of 42 minutes for 13 semi-structured interviews. The same questions were asked of all participants to include focus group participants, and the responses provided were sufficient in answering the research question posed by this study. Data saturation was determined to be a milestone in data collection in order to ensure there was sufficient data to answer the research question. This objective was achieved after the 10th interview was facilitated, and no new data was observed from three (3) additional interviews. To answer the research question posed by the gap in literature found in this study, an inductive thematic analysis approach was facilitated. This researcher utilized a six (6) step data analysis framework (Kiger &Varpio, 2020; Braun & Clark, 2006):

1. The familiarization of the data
2. Generation of initial codes
3. Search for themes
4. Review of themes
5. Defining and naming themes
6. Production of the report

Thematic analysis utilizing this six (6) step approach resulted in several themes emerging from the iterative process of coding and categorizing the data obtained from participants. Two research questions undergirded this study, and through a comprehensive data analysis process seven (7) themes ultimately manifested. Research Question one (1) explored the self-care techniques utilized by advocates in the prevention of compassion fatigue. Based on thematic analysis, four (4) themes developed from this question. Theme one: domestic violence advocates intentionally create boundaries between their work and personal life in order to prevent compassion fatigue, Theme two: domestic violence advocates use self-awareness as a self-care technique in the prevention of compassion fatigue. Theme three: domestic violence advocates utilize their colleagues and organizational leadership for support and accountability in the prevention of compassion fatigue. Theme four: domestic violence advocates take their holistic well-being into consideration in the prevention of compassion fatigue. Research Question two (2) explored about how domestic violence advocates use self-care to prevent compassion fatigue and out of data analysis three (3) themes were created. Theme five: Domestic violence Advocates utilize therapeutic strategies to prevent compassion fatigue in order to have a positive influence on the victims they serve.

Theme 6: domestic violence advocates utilize assorted self-care activities to ensure they maintain the longevity and quality of their professional life and prevent compassion fatigue. and Theme seven: domestic violence advocates engage in assorted therapeutic activities to prevent compassion fatigue.

This study identified limitations that emerged through data collection and the data analysis process. These limitations may have affected the interpretation of results, and impact trustworthiness of the data. There were three (3) semi-structured interviews that were truncated in length, in comparison to other participants. Although these interviews yielded data, despite follow up questions, and prompting for participant elaboration these three (3) participants were not as verbose and forthcoming in their responses as other participants. This researcher facilitated member checking in which study participants were sent each transcript with a request to review them for accuracy. However, this researcher did not include a summary or researcher interpretation of data, which may be considered a limitation of this study. In addition, this researcher did not engage in formal reflexivity protocols throughout thematic analysis and chose to utilize personal and peer reflexivity methods. Using these protocols did allow this researcher to self-examine throughout data analysis phases, this approach may be considered a limitation of this study. Limitations of this study will further be explored in Chapter 5.

In conclusion, the commencement of Chapter 4 provided an overview of what this chapter would entail. A comprehensive review of data analysis and the results of this study were given. This process included providing details related to descriptive findings, data analysis procedures, and the influence of trustworthiness on this study. Chapter 4 also presented the manner in which codes were obtained, catalogued and categorized into emerging themes. Subsequently, the results of data collected were provided at the conclusion of this chapter. Based on the information gleaned in Chapter 4, a comprehensive summary of this research study will be provided in Chapter 5. This chapter will include information related to the results of this research, limitations as documented by this researcher, and recommendations for future study. In addition, Chapter 5 will explore the strengths and weaknesses of this study, along with the theoretical and practical implications garnered from the data collected. Chapter 5 will conclude with recommendations for future research and practice based on the findings of this research study.

Chapter 5: Summary, Conclusions, and Recommendations
Introduction and Summary of Study

The purpose of this qualitative descriptive study was to study the influence of self-care in the prevention of compassion fatigue in domestic violence advocates. Domestic Violence is considered a major public health epidemic, in which advocates serve on the frontline providing support and resources to victims of domestic violence. In turn, advocates are exposed to compassion fatigue due their ongoing engagement with the trauma of victims of (Sansbury, Graves & Scott, 2015). Through a review of extant literature, it has been determined that self-care strategies are an essential (Bressi & Vaden, 2017) tool, in the prevention of compassion fatigue. Empirical data (Alani & Stroink, 2015, Merchant & Whiting, 2015, & Jones (2016), highlights the gap sought to be filled by this study, in the exploration of self-care strategies in domestic violence advocates in the prevention of compassion fatigue.

Elements of this study such as the research design, data collection approach and thematic analysis were aligned with a specific theoretical framework. It was determined that Orem's Theory of Self-Care, was the most suitable framework to undergird this research study, due to its focus on the examination of self-care practices (Allen, 2021). This study was conducted to elucidate this subject matter by adding to the body of knowledge pertaining to advocates, compassion fatigue and self-care. Along with a qualitative descriptive methodology, two research questions were considered foundational to understanding the phenomenon of this study.

RQ1: What self-care techniques do domestic violence advocates from the Mid-Atlantic region of the United States describe as typically being used in the prevention of compassion fatigue?

RQ2: How do domestic violence advocates from the Mid-Atlantic region of the United States use self-care to prevent compassion fatigue?

As an overarching goal Chapter 5 will encapsulate the summary of findings for this research study. In addition, practical implications as a result of this study, will be explored within this section. Chapter 5 will also delve into several recommendations for practical application of research findings, along with additional recommendations for future research.

Summary of Findings and Conclusion

Overall Organization

This section provides a synopsis of results from this study's thematic analysis, and subsequent findings. The theoretical framework that has underpinned this research and its alignment, will be reviewed along with extant supporting literature. The two research questions this study sought to understand, centered on describing the influence of self-care, in the prevention of compassion fatigue, in domestic violence advocates. In seeking to answer this study's research question it was determined that a descriptive approach would be considered most optimal. The findings from this qualitative descriptive research manifested through the responses provided by domestic violence advocates, who worked in local domestic violence organizations in the Mid-Atlantic region of the United States. Data was collected via semi-structured interviews and a focus group, with a total of 19 study participants. To guide the collection of this data, an interview protocol (Appendix I) was created by this researcher. Once responses were securely captured and data transcribed, along with member checking, iterative thematic analysis took place. Data evaluation to include coding, categorization and the emergence of themes, resulted in seven (7) themes manifesting in response to research questions which are provided in Table 8 in Chapter 4.

RQ1

The first research question inquired about the self-care techniques domestic violence advocates from the Mid-Atlantic region of the United States describe as typically being used in the prevention of compassion fatigue. Research question one provides the foundation for this study in engaging participants in dialogue as it pertains to self-care strategies and compassion fatigue. This question will provide the gateway response for the various types of self-care strategies that domestic violence advocates utilize. In addition, it will elucidate which self-care strategies are typically utilized and deemed most beneficial in the prevention of compassion fatigue.

Theme 1.1. Domestic Violence Advocates Intentionally create Boundaries Between Their Work and Personal Life in order to Prevent Compassion Fatigue. In response to questions related to self-care, participants expressed that clearly defined boundaries were an essential component in the prevention of compassion fatigue. Within the field of caring professions, the literature indicates that there is a deterioration of personal and professional life, without the careful consideration and implementation of demarcation (Page, 2021). Participants declared the importance of intentionally separating these two elements of their lives, which align with the ideology of Rimmer (2021), in the need to conscientiously demonstrate this division in self-care maintenance.

According to Smyth (2021), respecting boundaries is a reciprocal concept, wherein advocates reflected that they had to establish healthy boundaries with themselves, and also with their colleagues and victims served. Study participants could tell when their colleagues were not demonstrating self-care and at-risk of compassion fatigue, by their work habits and engagement in work assignments beyond the allotted work timeframes.

This theme as extracted from the data, correlates to findings in the literature that state when boundaries are left unchecked, the caring professional's well-being is negatively and wholistically impacted (Crivatu, Horvath, & Massey, 2021). Study participants shared the importance of maintaining a balanced work-life position, knowing that they cannot do everything served as a core value in the quest to maintain boundaries. This theme is also in congruence with the theoretical framework of this study as Orem's Theory of Self-care posits the intentionality that is needed in achieving self-care (Queirós, Silva, Cruz, Cardoso & Morais, 2021) as advocates in this study ascribed that they are learning to set healthy boundaries as an intentional act of self-care. Although study participants expressed that they may be perceived as selfish for engaging in self-care, they also recognized the need to put this work down and become self-focused as an essential boundary to implement.

Theme 1.2. Domestic Violence Advocates Use Self-Awareness as a Self-Care Technique in the Prevention of Compassion Fatigue. In the influence of self-care in the prevention of compassion fatigue, the theme of self-awareness elucidated how important advocate internal monitoring was in maintaining well-being. Study participants reported being in touch with themselves and the need to have an internal barometer dictating when self-care should be initiated. In this research advocates also shared that a lack of self-awareness can be a gateway for mental health deterioration and Zaretsky and Van Tassel (2021) posit that advocates should be self-aware enough to know when they are experiencing symptoms. Self-awareness is considered foundational as a strategy to diminishing the harmful effects of compassion fatigue in advocates (Crivatu, Horvath, & Massey, 2021). This thematic finding aligns with the research as Robino (2019), reported that compassion fatigue is more likely to be achieved when there is a lowered sense of self-awareness.

According to Adkins-Jackson, Turner-Musa, and Chester (2019), Orem's Theory of Self-care highlights that there must be an innate willingness to evaluate self, be intentional about health wellness, and put into practice consistent habits that augment self-care. Advocates proffered that they feel compelled to learn about themselves and knowing exactly when to take a break from advocacy work, and that this practice is a means to feeling less exhausted. In this study, Advocates shared that part of self-awareness related to being willing to ask for help and knowing where to go to get it. This principle aligns with this theme, and is further supported by Crivatu, Horvath, & Massey (2021) who state that instead of portraying a perception of competency, advocates who embody self-awareness, would be transparent in asking for help. Participants of this study shared how integral having self-awareness is as a strategy to preventing compassion fatigue, and that continuously learning about themselves served as a core-value in this process.

Theme 1.3. Domestic Violence Advocates Utilize Their Colleagues and Organizational Leadership for Support and Accountability in the Prevention of Compassion Fatigue. Within this theme study participants described that the support they receive from their co-workers, supervisors and leadership staff played an integral role in their self-care and compassion fatigue. From coworkers sharing the workload so advocates could self-care, to the culture of the organization surrounding self-care implementation, participants reported that these attributes dictated a healthy or unhealthy work environment. In the study conducted by Crivatu, Horvath and Massey (2021) it was found that organizational support more so than individual factors, played a greater role in removing the deleterious aspects of advocacy, such as compassion fatigue. In addition, the more organizational support given to advocates, the less likely they would experience the deleterious effects from victim trauma (Benuto, Singer, Gonzalez, Newlands, & Hooft, 2019).) Similarly in this study, mentorship, accountability, peer support and supervision were considered viable organizational intervention strategies that could help support fellow advocates practice self-care, in the prevention of compassion fatigue.

In Orem's Theory of Self-Care, this framework is best achieved in an environment that espouses the need for personal development (Martiningsih, Winarni, Acob, Baua, & Nugroho, 2021). This theme manifested in response to multiple participants sharing that when other advocates demonstrated poor self-care habits, that it negatively impacted the work environment. The literature (Farkas & Romaniuk, 2021; Zaretsky & Van Tassel, 2021) coincides with this theme, as participants reported how intentional their organization was in creating a workspace that embraces self-care.

Theme 1.4. Domestic Violence Advocates Take Their Holistic Well-Being into Consideration in the Prevention of Compassion Fatigue. This theme captured the multi-dimensional influence self-care had on participants. Advocates described how the lack of self-care impacted them beyond the professional arena. Participants discussed this imbalance, by sharing the physical, emotional, and personal toll of compassion fatigue. This theme was supported in the literature by researchers who shared the physical (Zaretsky & Van Tassel, 2021)), psychological (Crivatu, Horvath and Massey, 202; Pfaff, Freeman-Gibb, Patrick, DiBiase & Moretti, 2017) and familial impact (Crivatu, Horvath and Massey, 2021) that a lack of self-care has on advocates. Multiple participants shared that even in their personal time or in the community, they get pulled on to provide advocacy, support, and resources, wherein their professional lives bleed into their personal lives and cannot be turned off. This description augments research by Crivatu, Horvath and Massey (2021), that state that there is a duty to address the holistic wellbeing of such professionals. Research study participants expressed the domino effect that frequently manifests when one area of their life is out of balance, and that a comprehensive approach to this dilemma can help maintain the holistic well-being (Bressi & Vaden, 2017) of advocates.

RQ2

Research question two expounds upon the capacity in which self-care supports the prevention of compassion fatigue. While research indicates that self-care is vital to the prevention of compassion fatigue (Dorociak, Rupert, Bryant & Zahniser (2017), it would add to the body of empirical data to explore the magnitude to which self-care strategies genuinely influence the prevention of compassion fatigue within this population.

Theme 2.1. Domestic violence Advocates utilize therapeutic strategies to prevent compassion fatigue in order to have a positive influence on the victims they serve. This theme highlighted how participants described the influence their self-care had on the victims that they serve. Multiple participants expressed their dedication to the field of domestic violence, despite the resulting compassion fatigue they face. Participants were aware that their self-care can benefit or deleteriously impact victims who were already experiencing trauma and fragility. Zaretsky and Van Tassel (2021) validate this theme echoing that advocates compassion fatigue can result in decreased quality of client care and lack of engagement. (Benuto, Singer, Gonzalez, Newlands, & Hooft (2019), shares the helping professional level of client interaction, in addition to negatively impacting productivity and diminished decision making (Cocker & Joss, 2016). In this theme, participants affirmed what has been found in the literature promulgating that lack of advocate self-care translates to lack of client engagement and intervention, which ultimately affect treatment plan goals and objectives and the lives of victims served.

Theme 2.2. Domestic Violence Advocates Utilize Assorted Self-Care Activities to Ensure They Maintain the Longevity and Quality of Their Professional Life and Prevent Compassion Fatigue. Study participants spoke of the quality of professional of life as a theme, due to their desire to achieve career longevity. As a motivation to implement self-care, advocates for this study held firm to their desire to diminish the public health epidemic of domestic violence, as a career focus. This theme coincides with research by Cayir, Spencer, Billings, Hilfinger Messias, Robillard, and Cunningham (2021), on advocates and their self-care. It was determined that advocates were motivated to implement self-care by their desire to be help survivors, and be solution focused in addressing domestic violence prevention.

In addition, the literature validated this theme by stating that advocates were committed to the quality of their professional life by enacting social change, (Wood, 2014) and maintaining long-term work environment (Cayir et al.2021). Study participants also described the weight of the work they do and recognized that a misstep on their part could jeopardize the lives of victims. In this theme of maintaining the quality of professional life, participants emphasized the "WHY of the work" (Zaretsky and Van Tassel, 2021 p.73) advocates do, along with their purpose. Participants of this study reiterated their desire to remain in this field, and as such promote efforts towards well-being (Orem, 2021), as outlined by Orem's Theory of Self-Care.

Theme 2.3. Domestic Violence Advocates Engage in Assorted Therapeutic Activities to Prevent Compassion Fatigue. The theme of self-care techniques emerged as participants shared the assorted strategies utilized in the prevention of compassion fatigue. Study participants described the plethora of self-care modalities frequently engaged in, ranging from exercising, psychotherapy, nature to religious practices. Similarly, in their study of advocates Globokar, Erez and Gregory, (2019), participants shared that, boundaries, prayer, humor and being self-aware were all effective coping mechanisms used in their work with victims. The literature also proffered stress management sessions, yoga classes, a walking or a meditation group, or artistic activities (Zaretsky, L., & Van Tassel, B. 2021. P #) and exercising, healthy eating habits and consistent sleep patterns (Cayir et al.2021) as beneficial self-care techniques.

A participant of this study shared what could be categorized as a unique, literal, and symbolic self-care gesture. By washing hands after each client interaction, it demonstrated physically and psychologically, that they were washing away the emotional residue left over as a means of self-care. Within this theme, participants also stressed the importance of consistency, and intentionality as aligned with the literature (Beckerman, & Wozniak, 2018) as a standard practice in the deployment of self-care. Advocates in this study also acknowledged that they do not regularly implement self-care as often as they should, despite being aware of the benefits of self-care, in the prevention of compassion fatigue.

Research Questions Answered Based on Study Findings

Each of the research questions for this study, provided rich data in elucidating the influence of self-care, in the prevention of compassion fatigue, in domestic violence advocates, within the Mid-Atlantic region of the United States. In an effort to add to the body of knowledge, the gap as identified in the literature, was filled by this research. According to Benuto, Singer, Gonzalez, Newlands, & Hooft (2019), the current literature is lacking and has been neglectful pertaining to victim advocates and secondary traumatic stress, also considered compassion fatigue. In addition, Alani and Stroink (2015), support the need for future research on self-care within domestic violence advocates, as these helpers are exposed to compassion fatigue. In the study conducted by Alani and Stroink (2015), they provided a cursory examination of secondary traumatic stress, emotional exhaustion and burnout and the importance of addressing these factors as it relates to self-care within domestic violence advocates. Cocker and Joss (2016) also expose the gap in the literature as it relates to compassion fatigue and the strategies that may be utilized to address and diminish its occurrence. Merchant and Whiting (2015), suggest that further research on domestic violence advocates, who are considered frontline workers (An & Choi 2017), can result in a greater appreciation for the lived experience of advocates.

Orem's theory of self-care was selected as the theoretical framework used to help answer the research question posed by this study. According to Orem (2001), self-care entails engaging in practices that establish the maintenance of life, health, and well-being.

In their study Campbell & Soeken, (1999), utilized Orem's Theory of Self-Care as a framework to examine the self-care agency of battered women and its influence on their ability to maintain self-care. The findings from this study reveal that exposure to domestic violence can negatively impact self-care abilities. Domestic Violence Advocates are at high risk of compassion fatigue, and self-care strategies are seen as viable options in mitigating the occupational hazards faced by advocates. The purpose of this qualitative descriptive study is to describe the influence of self-care in the prevention of compassion fatigue in domestic violence advocates.

Describing the Phenomenon

The phenomenon this study sought to understand was how self-care influenced the prevention of compassion fatigue in domestic violence advocates from the Mid-Atlantic Region of the United States. Domestic violence is a public health epidemic, wherein domestic violence advocates provide support and resources to victims of domestic violence. In doing so, Advocates are exposed to the trauma of victims and subsequently suffer occupational hazards such as compassion fatigue. Self-care strategies are considered a viable intervention in the prevention of compassion fatigue. This study researched domestic violence advocates and how they described the influence of self-care in the prevention of compassion fatigue. Subsequently, this research sought to answer the research questions and determined the efficacy of descriptions utilized to address self-care in domestic violence advocates. Positionality- In assessing positionality within this study it was essential to consider the researchers worldview and how this construct could have influenced the outcome of the research conducted (Holmes, 2020). At the onset of this study, this researcher's professional employment was outside the scope of the profession this research sought to study. However, towards the latter portion of research conducted, this researcher was hired as a domestic violence advocate. This researcher's new position was not in alignment with those of this study who worked for domestic violence organizations. Instead, this researcher was hired to work within a different realm of domestic violence advocacy, that of law enforcement victim-based services.

While still working with those impacted by domestic violence, the functions of domestic violence organization advocates, and law enforcement domestic violence advocacy, were contrasted. In such a case, Holmes (2020) indicated that the researcher must ensure their lens do not skew, unduly influence nor compartmentalize the perspective of participants. As such, an ongoing exercise in reflexivity was conducted to assess this researcher's ability to clearly, critically, and transparently, facilitate this research (Secules, McCall, Mejia, Beebe, Masters, Sánchez-Peña, & Svyantek, (2021). This researcher intentionally processed and was aware of any bias, and reflexively diminished the potential to influence this study prior, and during each interview. While Holmes (2021) acknowledges that "there will always still be some form of bias or subjectivity" (p.4), this researcher facilitated best practice in reducing partiality, through the use of reflexivity.

Summary. As domestic violence is considered a public health epidemic (Macy, Martin, Nwabuzor Ogbonnaya and Rizo (2018)), advocates are needed to help victims. Therefore, it is essential to diminish the imprint of compassion fatigue, as an occupational hazard in this profession through the use of self-care. The findings of this research study, sought to add to the body of literature pertaining to the influence of self-care, in the prevention of compassion fatigue in domestic violence advocates. As such, the assorted implications of this research study are presented in the subsequent section.

Reflection on the Dissertation Process

In reflecting on the dissertation process, this researcher has determined that while the research process has been arduous, it has also been exceptionally rewarding. Significant scholarly progress has occurred in the achievement of alignment, iterative empirical data reviews, and the development of research findings. This section will highlight the areas of the dissertation process that require further reflection, such as the sampling process and data analysis.

Sampling Process. In reflecting upon the data collection sampling stage of this dissertation, I was under the impression that finding participants to engage in this research study would be a straightforward process. However, several variables presented as obstacles in gaining study participants, as data collection took place in the midst of the Covid-19 pandemic, during the Christmas/New Year season and with a population significantly stretched thin by the pandemic. The domestic violence community had experienced a surge in victims needing services, due to shelter in place mandates that left victims at heightened risk for incidents of abuse. This resulted in a greater need for domestic violence advocates to provide safety planning, services, and shelter for victims of domestic.

Recruitment took place during the holiday season when advocates were busy ensuring that resources were available for families to have safe Christmas. Each obstacle presented, made it challenging to proceed with data collection, however after much perseverance and patience, sufficient participants were recruited for this study. This researcher had to pivot and engage in snowballing sampling in addition to purposive sampling, which was originally proffered as this study's sampling method. Thankfully, advocates that did participate in this study recruited other advocates within their organization to participate, encouraging prospective participants to respond to this researcher's recruitment email. Participants were genuinely pleased that research was being conducted on their population, spotlighting the immeasurable work advocates do. In reflection of this dissertation process, it was inspiring to know that this research was contributing in efforts to make the lives of advocates easier.

Reflection on Data Analysis. Data analysis provided noteworthy opportunities for growth in learning how to facilitate thematic analysis. Initially, this process was to be conducted via software technology to assist with coding of the data collected. However, upon further reflection it was determined that for this scholar, researcher immersion in data coding would be the most viable option. It was assessed that this was the best approach for thematic analysis. Despite being a novice, this researcher was able to independently, explore the data collected, group categories and view themes as they emerged from the data.

This iterative process was helpful in enabling this researcher to hone skills that had not been utilized previously. While this process was time consuming and required this researcher to be detail oriented, further reflection reveals that as a novice researcher it was best to engage in the data analysis process at its most rudimentary level. Using this approach has served this researcher well, in preparation for future qualitative research opportunities.

Overall Reflection on the Dissertation Process. In reflection of this dissertation process, this researcher has been able to make significant scholarly progress and is pleased to make a noteworthy contribution in advancing scientific knowledge. While there were many challenges in the completion of this study, this researcher remains confident in the findings of research conducted overall.

Implications

This section of Chapter 5 presents the theoretical, practical, and future implications of this research study. Domestic Violence advocates are considered an underserved research group at risk to be exposed to compassion fatigue by the nature of this profession faced daily with victim trauma. (Benuto, Singer, Gonzalez, Newlands, & Hooft, 2019). The phenomenon this study sought to understand was how self-care influenced the prevention of compassion fatigue in domestic violence advocates from the Mid-Atlantic Region of the United States. In an effort to fill the gap found within literature, this qualitative descriptive study described the influence of self-care on domestic violence advocates in preventing compassion fatigue. In a review of literature, researchers highlighted that further research on domestic violence advocates (Merchant & Whiting, 2015), who are considered frontline workers (An & Choi 2017), can result in a greater appreciation for the lived experience of advocates. In filling the gap found within literature, this research has several implications pertaining to domestic violence advocates in the advancement of scientific knowledge. In addition, this researcher will examine the strengths and weaknesses as found in this study.

Theoretical Implications

The theoretical framework utilized to support this study was based on Orem's Theory of Self-Care (2001). This study adds to the theoretical knowledge base of this framework, by elucidating a research area unexplored, yet underpinned by this theory. The premise of self-care relates to engaging in practices that augment the maintenance of life, health, and well-being (Orem, 2001). According to, de Lima, dos Santos, Comassetto, de Oliveira, Correia and da Silva, (2017), Orem utilized the tenets of self-care and self-care deficit to outline a greater understanding of an individual's effort to achieve well-being.

This theory was used to understand the influence of self-care in the prevention of compassion fatigue in domestic violence advocates. In the application of this theory to this study's population, domestic violence advocates wellbeing and maintenance in the form of self-care was explored. In response to research questions, study participants shared their motivation for engaging in self-care, the decisions that influenced this commitment, and how it impacts construct and holistic functioning as domestic violence advocates. These results aligned with Orem's Theory of Self-Care, which asserted that each individual has the innate ability to maintain their equilibrium (Mohammadpour, Rahmati, Shahla, Khosravan, Alami, &Akhond, 2015; Wilson, 2017), and this study identified several themes that supported this effort by domestic violence advocates.

Overall, the results found in this study aligned with Orem's Theory of Self-care which dictated that each individual has the ability to engage in efforts to preserve and optimize their health, while diminishing behaviors that corrupt overall well-being (Maruca, Reagan, & Shelton, 2021). Participants described how they innately ascribed to maintaining their well-being, while demonstrating their motivation to prevent compassion fatigue. Overall, the themes derived from this study aligned with Orem's Theory of Self-Care which dictates that each individual has the ability to engage in efforts to preserve and optimize their health, while diminishing behaviors that corrupt overall well-being (Maruca, Reagan, & Shelton, 2021). Subsequently, participants described how they innately ascribed to maintaining their well-being, while demonstrating the motivation the prevention of compassion fatigue. Based on the information gleaned from participants, these findings can be added to the body of knowledge in congruence with this theoretical framework.

Practical Implications

There is significant literature on domestic violence and its impact as a public health epidemic, however, there is paucity of literature that focuses on domestic violence advocates, and even more scarcity of literature related to the occupational hazards they face and their self-care. As such, Alani and Stroink (2015), support the need for future research on self-care within domestic violence advocates (Cocker & Joss, 2016). This study sought to close the gap and add to empirical data related to the vulnerable population of domestic violence victims, and those that support and serve them. Several practical implications have manifested from this study's findings related to organizational structure and self-care, implications for new and seasoned advocates career longevity, and the overarching influence in diminishing the footprint of domestic violence on society at large.

Participants described the role that organizational leadership played in negating or bolstering advocate self-care. From this study, leaders of domestic violence organizations can learn how critical their role is in maintaining the holistic well-being of advocates under their leadership. With this proactive self-care stance from leadership, advocates will not fear reprisal or perceptions of ineptitude, when compassion fatigue sets in or self-care needs are prioritized. Leaders may ingrain within the culture of domestic violence organizations, self-care as a cornerstone for advocates individually and organization wide. This implication is further supported in the literature by Cayir, Spencer, Billings, Hilfinger Messias, Robillard and Cunningham (2020) who proffer that it is in the best interest of organizations to provide an environment that holistically fosters advocates well-being. With this benchmark solidified, another general implication from this study relates to the quality of professional services provided to victims. Participants of this study shared their motivation to engage in self-care, manifested from a desire to remain in the field of domestic violence advocacy, in a long-term capacity.

From a practical standpoint, this study can help prepare those entering the field of domestic violence advocacy with a greater understanding of how to prevent compassion fatigue. It can also bring attention to the occupational hazard frequently faced by advocates and motivate advocates to deploy self-care methodologies earlier. This study also, brings greater awareness to the field of domestic violence prevention. By adding to the body of literature, further attention is brought to this public health epidemic, as awareness saturation can help mitigate the effects of domestic violence and spur prevention. Based on these findings, organizations can implement a culture of self-care, advocates can lessen the effects of compassion fatigue, and awareness can be brought to domestic violence.

Future Implications

Through this research, domestic violence advocates provided insight on how they described the influence of self-care in the prevention of compassion fatigue. Future implications of the data yielded, are presented as a result of this study. In comparison to the study highlighted in Chapter 2 that was facilitated by Kulkarni, Bell, Hartman and Herman-Smith, (2013) on domestic violence service providers, they found that worker-organizational alignment of values and mission, served as contributing factors in countering compassion fatigue. Likewise, the findings of this study support the literature, as participants shared the integral role that their organizations played in supporting their self-care. Future implications may result in greater insight on organizational leadership and how to augment advocate self-care in the prevention of compassion fatigue.

Orem's Theory of Self-Care was utilized as the theoretical framework for this study. Traditionally utilized from a nursing perspective, this study expands the use of this theory broadening it beyond the scope of the nursing field. Future researchers may want to contribute to the literature by further expanding this theoretical framework to other helping professional fields. Participant's descriptions of the influence of self-care may produce further studies related to career longevity of advocates, frequently utilized self-care strategies efficacy, and the influence of leadership on organizational self-care implementation and maintenance. Several advocates also shared how integral their colleagues were in helping to balance the weight of caseloads, while holding advocates accountable in self-care implementation.

In addition, participants in this study described the challenges faced in establishing boundaries in attempt to engage in self-care. Subsequently, implications of this study could result in research to explore how advocates achieve boundaries, in establishing self-care and a work life balance. Studies with variations to this research would further elucidate this subject matter and bring greater understanding to the profession of domestic violence advocacy.

Strengths and Weaknesses of Study

Strengths

A noteworthy strength was this study's emphasis on domestic violence advocates, a population largely neglected within the body of research More research focus has been placed on understanding the phenomenon of domestic violence and batterer intervention programs (Hackett, McWhirter & Lesher, 2016), than on service providers such as domestic violence advocates, who strive to quell, intervene, and prevent further abuse. Addressing this subject matter within the literature, helps bring awareness, and augments a professional field on the front lines of domestic violence prevention. The qualitative methodology utilized in this study served as a strength, given its emphasis on meaning, interpretation (Gough & Lyons, 2016;) and multimodal data method (Boeren, 2018). In addition, the descriptive research design served as a strength in exploring phenomena that are not truly understood (Kim, Sefcik & Bradway, 2017), such as in the field of domestic violence advocacy.

A strength of this study was found in the rigor demonstrated by convening an expert panel, field testing, member checking and having an interview protocol in place. This multi-modal process helped solidify trustworthiness in ensuring that credibility, dependability, transferability, and confirmability were implemented within the confines of this study. Another strength identified within this study was the manner in which data analysis was conducted. This researcher utilized the iterative thematic approach as familiarized by Braun and Clarke (2006)

Through this intricate process, a rich and detailed data set (Majumdar, 2022), was obtained through the seven (7) themes that emerged in strengthening the findings of this research. Another noteworthy strength was that participants for this research study were spread out amongst four (4) different domestic violence organizations from the Mid-Atlantic region of the United States. This enabled broader and more diverse perspectives gleaned from participants, instead of a concentrated pool of participants that would have manifested if participants originated from only one domestic violence organization.

Weaknesses

Despite the plethora of strengths demonstrated within the body of this research, there were also notable weaknesses impacting the results of this study. A weakness, of this study related to focus group participants, as they all came from the same organization and worked with each other. It cannot be ascertained whether there was full transparency and veritable self-expression in response to research questions, as one of the participants was a supervisor. Full disclosure within the focus group related to self-care and compassion fatigue could have been impeded by participants for fear of being seen by other group members as weak or inept.

An additional weakness of this study centered on the sampling methods employed in this study. While a purposive sampling approach was initially utilized to obtain participants, this researcher segued to snowballing to recruit additional participants. These methods could have impacted study findings due to non-randomized selection of participants. An additional weakness of this study related to the sparsity of reflexivity and minimal use of member checking. While this researcher did use a modicum of reflexivity throughout this study as discussed in Chapter 4, tools such as audit trails, bracketing and reflective journaling (Eryilmaz, 2021) which serve to bolster trustworthiness were not utilized. Reflexivity provides the opportunity for there to be checks and balance diminishing researcher bias and preconceptions from infiltrating study results. This researcher did use personal and peer-review methods of reflexivity; however, these approaches are not considered as robust and reliable. Subsequently, this researcher's approach to reflexivity could serve as a weakness of this study. In addition, the use of member checking was utilized in this study, wherein each participant received a copy of their transcript for review. To further enhance member checking trustworthiness, a summary of the data as interpreted by the researcher along with the transcript would be sent to participants. This study did not incorporate this additional measure which could be seen as a study weakness. According to Holmes (2021), research is not precluded of some form of bias or subjectivity, as such, the aforementioned strengths, and weaknesses presented in this section, are notable aspects of this research study to consider.

Recommendations

This qualitative descriptive study sought to fill the gap in literature, as it relates to the influence of self-care in the prevention of compassion fatigue, in domestic violence advocates. The results of this research have been obtained by advocates working in domestic violence organizations in the Mid-Atlantic region of the United States. In closing the gap within literature through the fulfillment of this study, there are several recommendations pertaining to this phenomenon, that may need to be explored for further consideration.

Recommendations for Future Research

The following are recommendations for future research based on the findings extrapolated from this study:

1. A recommendation for future research stemming from this study, relates to broadening the sample population and methodology in future replicated studies. While this study limited the scope of advocates who could participate in this study to the Mid-Atlantic region of the United States, future research could expand the geographical spectrum. Having advocates participate in research from a larger territory would add to the depths of data collected and generate new ideas and concepts.

2. An additional recommendation for future research, relates to a change in methodological approach from qualitative, to mixed methods. Incorporating a statistical approach that examines the correlation and variables ascertained from numerical data associated with this subject matter, would advance scientific knowledge. A future mix-methods research study with regards to advocates and their self-care and compassion fatigue, would enlarge the sample size of such a study and add to the generalizability of findings.

3. This study highlighted domestic violence advocates and self-care strategies influence in the prevention of compassion fatigue. This research added to the body of scientific knowledge about advocates, who are an often neglected (Benuto, Singer, Gonzalez, Newlands, & Hooft, 2019) population researched within literature. Future research should explore other often overlooked helping professions self-care strategies, and prevention related to compassion fatigue. This research will elucidate other unrecognized professions that are exposed to victim traumas and create awareness in the prevention of compassion fatigue, wherein there is a dearth of literature.

4. Orem's Theory of Self-Care was utilized as the theoretical framework for this study, due to its context in understanding an individual's effort to achieve well-being (de Lima, dos Santos, Comassetto, de Oliveira, Correia and da Silva, 2017). Typically, utilized in research related to the nursing field, future research could explore using Orem's Theory of Self-care in non-medical fields of study, such as was conducted by this study on domestic violence advocates. The application of this framework beyond nursing and the field of domestic violence, would further advance scientific knowledge in this use of this theoretical framework and the understanding of well-being.

5. One of the themes highlighted by this study related to Colleague/Organizational Care, and future research could expound upon this theme. Participants in this study described the role organizational culture played in their self-care and compassion fatigue. Therefore, it is recommended that future research add to scientific knowledge by exploring in an in-depth manner how organizational culture and

leadership styles assuage or augment self-care and compassion fatigue in domestic violence advocates. This focus in research may re-examine organizational constructs and leadership emulation with regards to advocates self-care.

Recommendations for Future Practice

Domestic Violence is a major public health epidemic (Alvarez 2017; Arroyo, Lundahl, Butters, Vanderloo & Wood, 2017) that has far reaching, deleterious impact on society at-large. Advocates daily sacrifice their well-being bearing witness (Killian (2017) to the trauma faced by victims of domestic violence. As such, it essential that advocates implement self-care to diminish the influence of compassion fatigue. Based on the findings of this qualitative descriptive study, several recommendations for future practice are made and expounded upon.

The findings of this research can be of benefit to all domestic violence advocates, domestic violence organizations and their leadership, as well as anyone impacted by domestic violence. Future practice may examine the collaborative role that organizational culture, colleague support and leadership guidance play in maintaining advocate self-care and diminishing the effects of compassion fatigue. Participants expressed a determination to remain in the field of advocacy to help diminish domestic violence's impact on society. To maintain career efficacy and longevity, advocates must deploy self-care strategies to prevent compassion fatigue. Whereas, this research highlighted advocate self-awareness, and the need for self-care, participants reported not engaging in self-care regularly. Subsequently, advocates must reconcile the theoretical aspects of self-care, into practical implementation. This future practice will support advocates in successfully ameliorating the issues faced by domestic violence victims, while counteracting the effects of compassion fatigue.

Lehrner and Allen (2009) proffer that "domestic violence agencies are considered the backbone of the movement" (p.658) and in consideration of future practices, domestic violence organizations need to prioritize providing a supportive environment that embraces a genuine construct of self-care, that extends beyond lip-service. Leadership cannot tout the principles of self-care, while advocates suffer from compassion fatigue, fear reprisal, and being perceived as inept, for expressing challenges related to self-care. Future practice would provide opportunities for domestic violence leadership and advocates, to collaborate on innovative self-care strategies to be implemented organization-wide, which would support the quality of advocate professional life.

As indicated in Chapter 1 section related to advancing scientific knowledge and the significance of the study, there is limited data on the strategy used for the holistic care of domestic violence advocates, specifically related to compassion fatigue (Alani & Stroink, 2015, Merchant & Whiting, 2015, & Jones (2016). Based on the findings of this study a strategy emerged as evidenced by the themes pronounced within this study such as boundaries, self-awareness, and advocate self-care influence on victims. Future practice may include the role of intentionality in advocates deploying these principles in their practice of advocacy and self-care. Extrapolated from this qualitative descriptive study were seven themes that emerged from the data collected from advocates. These themes filled the gap found within literature and provided recommendations for future research and practice. Findings from this research study elucidated the descriptions of domestic violence advocates in the influence of self-care in the prevention of compassion fatigue.

www.ingramcontent.com/pod-product-compliance
Lightning Source LLC
LaVergne TN
LVHW011936070526
838202LV00054B/4675